YOU'RE THE PASTOR
NOW WHAT?

By

VIRGIL M. WOODS

EVANSTON, ILLINOIS

MAY, 2011

Table of Contents

Introduction

Unfortunately, oftentimes Pastors can be deemed unfit or incompetent when they fail to effectively grow and develop a church congregation, when in reality there are other dynamics that can strongly influence a Pastor's effectiveness, regardless of their individual aptitude. One of the inherent aspects of a connectional church is that pastors are often moved from one location to another. It is an annual process by which the Bishop appoints a clergyperson to serve as Pastor for one year. Each year the clergyperson must return to a conference and receive another appointment for the following year. Depending on the denomination, a pastor may or may not be moved at the sole discretion of the Bishop. Specifically, an African Methodist Pastor may not have the convenience of knowing they will be relocated no more than 3-5 days in advance. It is common practice to receive a new appointment on Saturday and be expected to show up at the new charge the following day. These dynamics present unique challenges for both seasoned and nonseasoned African Methodist pastors as they are repeatedly called to establish a new working relationship with an existing congregation.

This study is focused on how a pastor positions oneself at the onset of his new charge in order to better his or her chances of being a successful and fulfilled pastor. In essence, this study is the precursor to church growth books. By focusing on the Pastor's development clergy will be able to better ascertain what may or may not work as they read these books and sift through the vast array of suggestions the current literature offers.

When I began this study I had one question in mind: What does an African Methodist Pastor need to know coming into a new relationship with an existing congregation? I started by reading some of the more popular books geared towards church growth. Rick Warren's *Purpose Driven Church*[1] spoke more about starting a

---

[1] Rick Warren. *The Purpose Driven Church*. (Grand Rapids, Zondervan, 1995).

new church and less about transitioning into an existing one. Others like *I Refuse to Lead a Dying Church²*, *Church Unique³*, *The Emotionally Healthy Church⁴* and *The Passion Driven Church⁵*, all assume a pastor congregation relationship is already in existence. Though they are great books and contain some principles which we will visit in this study, none of them spoke specifically to the first year experience. I then decided to look at some of the corporate management literature, specifically three well-known titles: *You're In Charge, Now What⁵*, *The First 90 Days⁶* and *The New Leaders' 100-Day Action Plan⁸*. These works offered wonderful suggestions, some of which will be referenced later, but they suffered major contextual issues with regard to ministry. Objectives such as upward mobility and immediate success don't translate well with regard to church and the mission of the Pastor. Please note, that all of these works offer helpful suggestions and advice in their own right, but again, none of them were tailored to or targeted the first year experience. There are other works that do speak to the first year clergy experience, but my research will zone in on the African Methodist Episcopal Church and specifically, first year experiences within such framework.

This official study started with my third charge, Allen Chapel in Rockford, IL, which has been in existence since 1891 and has seen 22 pastors during this 109 year period. There are a group of approximately 90 members in this congregation who have enjoyed, or survived, numerous leadership changes over the last five decades. They retain a wealth of knowledge with regard to the do's and don'ts for a Pastor coming into an existing congregation,

---

² Paul Nixon. *I Refuse to Lead a Dying Church*. (Cleveland, Pilgrim Press, 2006).

³ Will Mancini. *Church Unique*. (San Francisco, Jossey-Bass, 2008).

⁴ Peter Scazzero. *The Emotionally Healthy Church*. (Grand Rapids, Zondervan, 2003). ⁵ Kent M. Millard and E. Carver McGriff. *The Passion Driven Congregation*. (Nashville, Abingdon Press, 2003).

⁵ Thomas J. Neff and James M. Citrin. *You're In Charge—Now What?* (New York, Three Rivers Press, 2005).

⁶ Michael Watkins. *The First 90 Days*. (Boston, Harvard Business Review Press, 2003). ⁸ George B. Bradt, Jayme A. Check and Jorge E. Pedraza. *The New Leader's 100-Day Action Plan*. (Hoboken, John Wiley & Sons, Inc., 2009).

particularly during the first year. They have also formed a number of opinions regarding what makes an effective Pastor and what they, as lay members, look for in a new arrival. Wanting to dig deeper into their expectations of a new arrival, I began this study with an online survey soliciting their input.[7] This study then expanded by welcoming input from others including Pastors[8] and lay persons who operate in a similar connectional system. I also decided to interview a few pastors to gain more input. Dozens of lay members were surveyed from a variety of denominations and a select handful of Pastors were personally interviewed, some of whom will be mentioned, some who will not. Though this study cannot accurately say that it received input from *every* denomination, I can comfortably say that many church sizes and demographic makeups are represented here; from the small church to the mega church; from Baptist to Methodist to Non-denominational and a few things in between. However, the majority of the data came from African-American church members in African Methodist Episcopal Churches. The other recognized bias is the fact that participation required going online and this may have slightly skewed the data by limiting senior member's ability to respond, though some were still able to.

As I collected data, I began to reflect on my own ministry experiences. My first church was Bethel AME Church, Clinton, Iowa. It was a rural family church with 35 members. When I left two years later, our average Sunday attendance was slightly over 100 people. My second charge was Grant AME Church in Toronto, Ontario, Canada. It was a metropolitan church with an average Sunday attendance of 150 people. After two years, we were seeing more than 300 people on Sunday morning. My third and current position is with Allen Chapel AME Church in Rockford, IL. Upon my arrival in 2004, we had 65 very devoted members. Our membership roll now exceeds 400 and we are celebrating five years in our new 32,000 square-foot facility. I have successfully established and rejuvenated three healthy ministries in two

---

[7] See Appendix 3
[8] See Appendix 2

countries and three completely different social settings. These experiences formed a Participatory Action Research[9] with each —first year‖ representing another action cycle. So, I asked myself, what lessons did this early experimentation yield that might inform this study?

The survey responses and data, along with the interview information, was then compiled and analyzed for reoccurring themes and propensity toward certain responses. I reflected and infused my personal research data and finally, conclusions were drawn.

This project focused on this crucial first year of relationship development as it sought to extrapolate key points of formation in hope of empowering Pastors to come into existing congregations with their best foot forward. I have provided grassroots practical instruction based on my years of learning and experience, and the data and information found in this study. The results have been categorized into six major sections. *How We Prepare Ourselves* discusses taking advantage of the days before you officially begin in the new position. *How We Power Ourselves* examines the importance of spiritually undergirding yourself and preventing clergy burnout. *How We Present Ourselves* follows the old adage of —first impressions are everything.‖ *How We Position Ourselves* is an introduction to discovering the culture of your church. *How We Promote Ourselves* raises the importance of hospitality. Finally, *How We Preach*, offers some practical words to help pastors become better preachers.

Bishop John Richard Bryant, Senior Bishop of the African Methodist Episcopal Church and once pastor of a multi-thousand member church in Baltimore, Maryland, shared these words with me. When asked, "How do you continue to grow when you find yourself plateauing or hitting a glass ceiling?" he responded, "I had to constantly reinvent myself."[10] He did not say he reinvented the

---

[9] See Appendix 1

church, as many of us attempt to do. He said that we must reinvent ourselves. Though this study is written with a focus on the first year of ministry in an existing congregation, the principles and insights shared here can be informative, transformative and just as effective for *any* church leader who is at a place where he is ready to reinvent himself[11].

Read it in prayer and may God continue to bless you real good!

---

[10] Bishop John R. Bryant. Personal Conversation with Author. March 2009. Rockford, Illinois.
[11] I will use the single male pronoun "he" for the sake of simplicity while writing. However, know that I strongly believe God uses whom God chooses, male or female.

HOW WE PREPARE OURSELVES

Introduction

As a pastor called to a new church, you are about to embark on a new journey. How well you do on the journey will not only be determined by the decisions you make during the journey, but also how well you are prepared before the journey begins. When we watch athletic events we see athletes perform with amazing efficiency and grace as they confront their respective challenges. What we do not see is the hours of preparation that preceded the event. Their work doesn't start at the tip-off or the opening whistle; it starts months before they arrive for the game. You may not have the benefit of knowing about your new position months in advance, but whatever time you have, it is important that you use it wisely as you prepare. The game starts before the game starts. Thomas Neff, author of *You're In Charge, Now What*, calls this the countdown period.[12] It is the time between when you find out you have the new position and the day you actually take the position. He states —all countdown periods share a common goal: to learn as much as possible about the new world you're about to enter so that you can figure out how to best explore and navigate your way through it‖[13] when you get there. In this section we will talk about using the countdown period in three ways: learn the course, learn from yourself and prepare your family.

Learn the course.

When we see pro golfers take the tee on Thursday to start what usually is a four-day tournament, this is not the first time they have played the course. They are given the benefit of playing practice rounds in the days prior. It is the job of the golfer and the caddie to take extensive notes as to the nuances of the golf course. Where

---

[12] Thomas J. Neff and James M. Citrin. *You're In Charge, Now What?* (New York: Three Rivers Press, 2005), 19.

[13] Thomas J. Neff and James M. Citrin. *You're In Charge, Now What?* (New York: Three Rivers Press, 2005), 19.

are the hazards? What angles are best to approach the flag from? What is the grass or surface like? Is it a windy course or a calm course? All of this data will influence the golfers approach. Those who are aware of the challenges before they occur are best prepared to deal with them. It is no different for us as Pastors. Though we are not able to play practice rounds before we take the position, we can tap into some key points of information prior to our first day in the office. As we do this, we want to take note of what challenges we may be facing before we get there.

Dr. Kenneth Board is the pastor of Pilgrim Baptist Church in Illinois. He moved only a few years ago from Atlanta, Georgia. He shared with me some of his —learning the course‖ process during the countdown period in the following excerpt: —I got on the internet and looked during that time….census, the Chamber of Commerce, the Visitors and Tourism Bureau; I looked at that kind of

statistical data to get a sense of the city.‖[14]

Rev. DeCarto Draper, senior pastor of Providence Baptist Church expounded upon his use of the countdown period as well: —I have such a vast array of guys across this country, I called guys that I knew, that knew about the church, knew people in the church and ironically, I had a member in my first church who has family in this church and so they were able to give me a little insight. And then, you research the previous Pastors if you know any of them, and I did know some of the previous pastors so I could get a feel for the church through them.‖[15]

The interviews revealed four major sources of information at your disposal. Use these sources to help you learn the course. You have the internet, your predecessor, officers or veteran members and your colleagues.

---

[14] Kenneth Board. Interviewed By Author. Rockford, Illinois, Feb 3, 2011.
[15] DeCarto Draper. Interviewed By Author. Rockford, Illinois. Feb 10, 2011.

Your first source is the internet. The internet has made gathering data amazingly easy and efficient. You should have no problem finding the size and geographic location of the city you will be working in. Is the church located downtown where parking may be an issue? Is the church located in a rural town or in a remote location where it may be hard to find? Larger cities often offer a larger pool of human resources with regard to musicians and staff. Larger cities tend to have more elaborate public transportation systems. Is the church on a bus route? Is the church on a major road or intersection where it is easily visible? Are there other major landmarks near the church that may help people identify its location?

In 2002, I was appointed Pastor of Grant African Methodist Episcopal Church in East Toronto, Ontario, Canada. An online satellite image gave me a glimpse of my first major issue. The church was a beautiful edifice that could seat over seven hundred people comfortably. However, it was located near downtown and the satellite image revealed that it was completely encompassed by houses and buildings. There was no parking lot. I also discovered that the train ran directly in front of the church; this was definitely beneficial. I began to wonder how many people came to church on the train as a result of the lack in parking. Later, I discovered that many did use the train and this fact was confirmed when I attempted to implement an 8am morning service-- a growing practice in the USA. The trains did not start running until 9am on Sunday and the majority of the people said they would not be able to make it. I was not surprised because I was already keenly aware of the situation before I got there. It also explained to me why Sunday School could start no earlier than 9:30am.

In my home town of Des Moines, Iowa, QuikTrip is one of the largest convenience store chains in the area. QT, as it's called, has an interesting marketing strategy. Every store they own or open is located on the corner of a major intersection. QT understands that having a good product is one thing, getting people

3

to it is another. Much of their success is attributed to a high degree of visibility and accessibility. This concept also applies to your church.

Having used the internet, you can now begin to think about how you will market your church, the ease with which it is incidentally seen and, ultimately, how people will get there. This is only one example of using the internet. As you gather more geographic and demographic information you will find other areas of focus besides location. Remember, at this point we are only drawing mental pencil sketches and formulating initial ideas.

A second source of information during your count down period is your predecessor. If your predecessor is available to you, it is imperative that you take time with them to discuss the makeup and challenges of the church as you learn the course. Please note, that depending on why your predecessor is leaving, he (or she) may or may not be cooperative in this area. However, if your predecessor is willing to talk, this conversation can be a valuable resource.

Pastor George Moore was retiring at age 78 when I arrived at Allen Chapel AME Church in Rockford, Illinois. We went to lunch and he began to share with me the church's desire to build a new facility. He explained to me that the church had been inundated with a number of building campaigns going back three pastors before him. In other words, another building campaign would probably be met with opposition. This was good to know since I was already aware of the churches desire for a new building. He also warned me of certain individuals who oftentimes had ulterior motives. When I arrived the first week I was greeted by a lady who handed me a list of names. —These are the people who need to be officers in the church and since you are new, I thought I would help you by making this list,‖ she explained. I knew that she was one of those that my predecessor had mentioned and I was not surprised to find her own name at the top of that list.

4

I am not suggesting that you buy into everything your predecessor says blindly and wholeheartedly. I am suggesting, however, that they can alert you to certain hazards that may exist.

When I arrived at my first church, Bethel AME Church in rural Clinton, Iowa, I was told by my predecessor that the financial secretary was very difficult to work with and really needed to be replaced. I took note of this, but I also wanted to make that decision based on my own observations. After a few weeks and a few conversations, I found that the financial secretary was very competent in her area, and I also discovered the source of tension. It seems that she was an impeccable record-keeper, but my predecessor did not keep credit card receipts. She remained my treasurer for the two years I was there, and she is still my friend to this day.

Though the predecessor can be a valuable source, you have to be careful not to reach conclusions prematurely and solely based on the information they provide. Just because someone did not get along with your predecessor doesn't mean he or she will not get along with you or serve well in the position. Do not be surprised when members who have been labeled cantankerous or difficult are actually very pleasant. You may not be the only one who is trying to reinvent yourself. Leave room for grace and don't hold them hostage to their reputation of the past.

A third resource is your officers and long standing members. They will be able to articulate the successes and failures of the years prior to your arrival. They may articulate the hopes of the congregation and the expectations they have of you as a new arrival.

When I received my appointment to Allen Chapel, I was in Chicago, Illinois, and four of the church officers were there to greet me. I asked them how many were attending Sunday service and they said sixty five. I asked them about the building and they said they were ready for a new one. It was a short and simple conversation that proved to be insightful. We discussed the previous pastors and I discovered that the average tenure for the last three pastors was about ten years. This told me that this was going to be a place I could stay a while. I could also tell that they were accustomed to very good preaching and that if I was going to succeed I would have to strengthen myself in this area.

It is important to note that in my research almost every Pastor suggested moving cautiously when listening to church members at the beginning of your appointment. Members often present themselves as how they want you to see them, not who they really are, and thus they tell you what you want to hear, not what you need to hear. It bears repeating: move slowly when talking with members. —It's not that people lie about what's important to them. It's just that value statements and creeds are often aspirational. You must understand the resting, steady state norms of attitudes, behaviors, and communication that people default to when the boss is not around.‖[16] This takes time.

A final source for count down information can come from your colleagues, particularly if you are in a connectional church system. Your colleagues can give insight into the history of the church. I would discover through my colleagues that Allen Chapel was a place that was accustomed to having the Bishop visit and though it was a small church, it was held in high regard because of its rich history. I also found that it wasn't always this small, and that in the early _80s it was a very thriving congregation whose pastor would later move on to become a General Officer in the church. In other words, though we were small we were not off the radar. This was great. I now knew that even though I was not at a —large‖ church or in a major city, per se, any successes I achieved here would not go unnoticed and could be beneficial to my career in the long term.

---

[16] George B. Bradt, Jayme A. Check and Jorge E. Pedraza. *The New Leader's 100 Day Action Plan*. (New Jersey, Wiley & Sons, 2009), 94.

Learning the course is an important phase because you will not be able to focus on everything in the beginning. The information you get here will allow you to tailor your focus and approach in the first year as you develop your plan for success.

Learn From Yourself

—The countdown period is the ideal time to assess not just the situation, but your own skills. Do you have the knowledge and network necessary to meet the challenges you've identified? Be brutally honest, your success depends on it."[17]

As you begin to go into your new charge it is wise to reflect upon the lessons you have learned about yourself along life's way. These lessons will highlight key growing opportunities as you go into your first church or new congregation. What inadequacies did you discover within yourself from the last experience, be it work or school? What personal areas would you like to strengthen as you come into your new position?

Transitioning into your new congregation is the prime time to reinvent yourself, focus on strengths and compensate for weaknesses. For example, if you've led a congregation before, you probably know that there is nothing more frustrating than leading a group of people who have an inaccurate perception of you. Now is the chance to ask yourself: what did you do to make them think that way? And more importantly, how can you change your behavior in the new charge so that congregants get a truer picture of who you are. You want to use your first year to begin developing the image you want them to have of you. We will discuss this further in *How We Present Ourselves*.

I learned this lesson first hand. When I arrived at Allen Chapel, I immediately saw the need for more young people in the church. Based on the average age of the current membership, we

---

[17] Thomas J. Neff and James M. Citrin. *You're In Charge, Now What?* (New York: Three Rivers Press, 2005), 32.

7

were ten to fifteen years from becoming extinct. I began to work with the music department as we incorporated a good amount of contemporary music into our Sunday Service. I began to talk about the need to bring young people to church and create an environment that was attractive to a younger demographic. It was not long before it was said that the new young pastor doesn't like traditional music and doesn't care for —old‖ people. I was shocked! Au contraire, the traditional music of the church is actually my favorite and I have always seen senior members as an invaluable source of information and inspiration. This first impression has taken me years to change and its effects are still lingering. As I looked back at the presentations and the language I used to try to get the congregation to catch my vision, I realized that I had painted a wonderful picture, but I had excluded the veteran members. This was a lesson well learned. My actions had caused my congregants to think of me in a way that simply was not true. The lesson: Be careful in how you present your vision and yourself.

If I were to move to a new charge, I would definitely make sure my vision was conveyed in a way that was much more inclusive and allowed congregants to see more clearly who I am and what I loved about the current setting. Language is an area I would work on. What about you? What areas are you willing to work on going into your new position? This is a prime opportunity to reinvent yourself.

Preparing Your Family

Most of the time, taking a new church requires moving to a different city. I cannot stress enough the importance of having your family on board. For a Pastor, when home is not right, nothing will be. Neff writes, —Planning to take on a new leadership role is not only about preparing yourself. It requires thinking about how your new phase will impact your family and other members of your personal support team. You need them to understand and buy into what will be necessary for your new assignment. This is always a delicate balancing act, recognizing that for a period of time things will be out of whack, requiring more effort on their parts as well as yours, until you can all reach a new equilibrium."[18]

Though your sacrifice will be great, theirs will be greater. You are excited about the new church, you are excited about reinventing yourself, and you are excited about what opportunities may lay ahead. Your family, on the other hand, may have a completely different perspective. They may be losing friends that they have come to love. Your spouse may be looking for a new job or leaving a department in the church she enjoys. Your children will now be the new kids on the block when they arrive at school. You must be conscious of these residual anxieties and work to make the transition as smooth as possible. Give your family opportunities for input. If they are old enough, talk to the children about the school district you are moving to and listen to what concerns they have or what may be most important to them. Prayerfully, your spouse is aware and supportive of your career choice and relocation expectations are not a total surprise. You may not have all of the answers and be able to fix every problem and concern. However, when you give your time and attention to your family, it will reiterate your love and commitment to your family and assure them that they will not be forsaken in the transition.

Conclusion

During the countdown period you will discover the beauty of your new landscape. Be careful though, you don't want to draw concrete conclusions at this point. You may find that some things are not exactly as they seem once you get to the location. Viewing images of the church and community is, however, a good way to start your creative juices flowing as you prepare for the journey.

---

[18] Thomas J. Neff and James M. Citrin. *You're In Charge, Now What?* (New York: Three Rivers Press, 2005), 35.

Take advantage of the internet, your predecessor, long standing members, colleagues and any other source of information at your disposal. Begin to reflect upon your personal strengths and weaknesses as you seek to grow in your new position. Prepare your family for the transition.

A good amount of preparation at this level will give you a strong advantage in being effective your first year and the years to come.

HOW WE POWER OURSELVES

Introduction

Your spiritual health is very important, not only for the sake of eternal life, but vocationally as well. How important is it to your success as a Pastor? Listen to the words of Peter Scazzero, author of *The Emotionally Healthy Church*. —The overall health of any church or ministry depends primarily on the emotional and spiritual health of its leadership. In fact, the key to successful spiritual leadership has much more to do with the leader's internal life than with the leader's expertise, gifts, or experience.‖[19] Dr. James Miller, Pastor of DuPage AME Church in Illinois, has experienced growth from a few hundred to over two thousand members. In his book, *Go Build A Church*, he writes, —As soldiers on the spiritual battlefield, we must always be aware that we are subject to attacks from the devil, our spiritual adversary...setting priorities and practicing disciplines serve to undergird us as we continue in Christian service.‖[20] It is this spiritual undergirding toward which we now turn our discussion. It is important for you to understand that it is easier to develop good spiritual habits during the first year as you formulate your new work ebb and flow than it is to squeeze them in after the fact.

Clergy Burnout

CNN Money provided a list of the top 15 stressful jobs that pay poorly.[21] Minister was ranked number 10. The demands of a minister can be grueling, stressful and oftentimes, for a lack of a better word, insane! Any profession that has to deal with people's personal issues and requires that you continually interact with people during the lowest points of their lives will eventually take its

---

[19] Peter Scazzero. *The Emotionally Healthy Church* (Grand Rapids, Zondervan, 2003), 20.

[20] James F. Miller. *Go Build A Church!* (Enumclaw, WinePress Publishing, 2007), 199.

[21] http://money.cnn.com/galleries/2009/pf/0910/gallery.stressful_jobs/10.html

toll on you. In addition, as much as a minister may try, this vocation has no set hours. You may be called at 2 a.m. to come to the hospital or visit the family of a recently deceased member. You will be called to facilitate funeral services at unexpected times as death is no respecter of calendar or schedule. At best, you may get a one-week notice and be expected to carve out a minimum of half a day for the home-going service, notwithstanding the time you will need to prepare the eulogy. And of course you will still be expected to deliver a fresh, inspiring and powerful sermon every seven days for the rest of your career, or at least until you equip some help. Simultaneously, you will be expected to buy girl scout cookies, write a letter of recommendation, visit the sick, take communion to the shut-in, go to graduation, stop by the baby shower, and attend community functions, banquets and events, and...ok...you get the point. I'm not saying that any of this is bad, only that in its totality, it can be very demanding. It is for this reason that you must undergird yourself spiritually for the journey.

Clergy burnout is a reality. When looking at the three reasons Dr. Carlyle Stewart III, renowned Senior Pastor of the multi-thousand member Hope United Methodist Church of Southfield, Michigan, offers regarding clergy burnout, I can personally say I have been guilty.[22] First, though I would never see myself as a messiah, I have clearly tried to live up to —messianic expectations.‖ Second, I have often compromised certain decisions because I knew I was living in the fish bowl and all eyes were on me. Third, yes, I have tried to fill every role that comes my way, from realtor to HVAC expert to preacher to counselor to father to husband. Yes, Dr. Stewart III, I am three times guilty of —not taking enough time to rest, relax, and have fun.‖[23] I have met clergy burnout face to face and it is not a pretty sight, but in such a busy world with so much to do, and a crowded

[22] Carlyle Stewart III. *Quarterly Review: A Journal of Theological Resources for Ministry*, Spring 2003, Article Titled: "Why Do Clergy Experience Burnout?" 78.
[23] Carlyle Stewart III. *Quarterly Review: A Journal of Theological Resources for Ministry*, Spring 2003, Article Titled: "Why Do Clergy Experience Burnout?" 80.

Microsoft Outlook Calendar, how can one ever find room for personal spiritual development? The words of the Merovingian from the movie *The Matrix Reloaded* come to mind, —How can one ever *have* time if one doesn't *take* time?!‖[24]

How the church operates, how the church sees the role of the Pastor, how the church sees itself, your spiritual disciplines, your walk with God, and your physical health are all interrelated.

You will love the church very much and you will want to see people helped through the awesome power of God. This may be why your level of commitment is so high, along with your fervor for work. However, at risk of reoccurring clergy burnout, the question must change in your mind. What begins as —What more can I do for the church?‖ has to become —What is in the best interest of the church?‖ The former insinuates a proactive approach to success and productivity. The latter leaves room for the understanding that sometimes less can produce more. If taking a rest in order to rejuvenate one's self causes you to perform more efficiently and more effectively, then this means fewer office hours actually leads to more work getting done, i.e. greater productivity. It is important that you understand this concept so you do not —feel guilty‖ when you take a rest. By resting you <u>are</u> being more productive. As a matter of fact when I conversed with Doug Thiesen, a lead pastor of the 8,000 member Heartland Community Church in Rockford, Illinois, he expressed that taking the break was not the most difficult part. It is taking the break —without feeling guilty‖ that is tough.[25] Don't feel guilty! Avoiding clergy burnout is an essential part of growing yourself and growing the church.

---

[24] The Matrix Reloaded. DVD. Warner Brothers Entertainment. Copyright 2003.

[25] Doug Theisen. Interview by Author. Heartland Community Church, Rockford, Illinois, February 8, 2011.

Spiritual Disciplines

One of the best ways to spend a break and avoid clergy burnout is spiritual disciplines. Marjorie J. Thompson, author of *Soul Feast*, offers this concise definition of spiritual disciplines: ―Spiritual Disciplines are practices that help us consciously to develop the spiritual dimension of our lives.‖[26] When we think of the word ―discipline‖ we often think of rigorous exercises or some type of military regiment. In this case, discipline actually refers to a conscious and intentional effort to draw closer to God. It can be a regiment or exercise, but it doesn't have to be. There is a wide array of disciplines that one can participate in and ultimately, it is incumbent upon the individual to discover what is most fruitful for them. In other words, there is no exact right or wrong with regard to spiritual disciplines. The only wrong would be not having any spiritual disciplines in place. Howard Thurman shares valuable insight regarding spiritual disciplines in his book *Disciplines of the Spirit*. He writes,

> The true purpose of all spiritual disciplines is to clear away whatever may block our awareness of that which is God in us. The aim is to get rid of whatever may so distract the mind and encumber the life that we function without this awareness, or as if it were not possible. It must be constantly remembered that this hunger may be driven into disguise, may take a wide variety of twisted forms; but it never disappears—it cannot. Prayer is the experience of the individual as he seeks to make the hunger dominant and controlling in his life. It has to move more and more to the central place until it becomes a conscious and deliberate activity of the spirit. When the hunger becomes the core of the individual's consciousness, what was a

---

[26] Marjorie J. Thompson. *Soul Feast* (Louisville: Westminster John Knox Press, 1995), 9.

sporadic act of turning toward God becomes the
very climate of the soul.‖[27]

As talk about spiritual disciplines and the importance of
creating spiritual time in order to prevent burnout, we will look at
three areas: personal challenges, procedural challenges and
perspective challenges. It is important that you understand their
interrelatedness.

Personal Challenges

Prayer Time

Many Christians traditionally pray a morning and night prayer and
their daily prayer life is emergency driven. Have you tried to
increase the frequency of your prayer time and also the length of
your prayer time. I call it prayer *time* because much of prayer time
is spent not always praying, in the traditional sense of talking to
God. Instead, it is often meditation and applying the principles of
Centering Prayer as outlined by Dwight Judy in *Christian Meditation
and Inner Healing*.[28] The fact that Judy calls it prayer is only to
provide language, it really is more of a *nothing*, or more explicitly it
is a letting-go. Admittedly, you may fall asleep sometimes, or find
your mind drifting, but I have found good spiritual fruit there and
operate with the expectation that I will get better as time goes on.
As a leader, especially in the first year, it is important that you are in
tune with the direction the Holy Spirit is leading. This comes from
prayer time.

When I was pastoring my first church, I asked a pastor,
whom I respected very dearly, the following question: —What do

---

[27] Howard Thurman. *Disciplines of the Spirit*. (Richmond, Indiana: Friends United Press,
1963), 96.
[28] Dwight H. Judy. Christian Meditation and Inner Healing (Akron: OSL Publications,
2000), 92.

you think is the key to success for a Pastor?‖ He replied, ―Son, there are three things that you need-- prayer, prayer and more prayer.‖ At first, this sounded more like a novel Sunday School answer than the sincere advice I was seeking. Years later, as you can tell, I still remember his words… and how correct he was. I believe every pastor ought to receive knee pads along with their clergy collar at ordination because you will find yourself praying that much. Think, for just a moment, how often Jesus prayed during his ministry. Richard J. Foster offers this cursory glimpse in *Streams of Living Water*:

> ―Like a recurring pattern in a quilt, so prayer threads its way through Jesus‗ life. As Jesus was baptized by John, he ―was praying‖ (Luke 3:21). In preparation for the choosing of the Twelve he went up the mountain alone and ―spent the night in prayer‖ (Luke 6:12). After an exhausting evening of healing ―many who were sick‖ and casting out ―many demons,‖ Jesus got up early in the morning ―while it was still very dark…and went out to a deserted place, and there he prayed‖ (Mark 1:35). Jesus was ―praying alone‖ when he was prompted to ask his disciples, ―Who do you say that I am?‖ (Luke 9:18-20). When Jesus took Peter, James, and John ―up on the mountain to pray,‖ it lead to the greatest transfiguration experience, and Luke notes that the appearance of Jesus‗ face was changed ―while he was praying‖ (Luke 9:2829). After the disciples had failed to heal a sick child, Jesus took care of the matter for them, explaining their failure in these words: ―This kind can come out only through prayer‖ (Mark 9:29). Jesus‗ fiercest anger came when he saw how people had turned the temple, which he said was to be a house of prayer, into a den of robbers (Matt.

21:13). It was after Jesus finished —praying in a certain place‖ that the disciples asked him to teach them to pray (Luke 11:1).[29]

There is much literature on prayer that goes beyond the scope of this study. Let it suffice for this conversation, to see prayer in its simplest form—conversation with God.

When we watch NFL football games, we always see the Head Coach standing on the side line wearing those huge headphones. You ever wonder who they are talking to? They are talking to the guys/gals in the booth at the upper level of the stadium. Why? Because the folks in the booth have a vantage point that allows them to see things the coach cannot see from the ground. This added information given to the coach, allows him to make the best decision considering the circumstances. It is no different with God. There are some things that only God knows and only God can see. Use those spiritual headphones and talk to God. One of the greatest benefits of prayer is that it allows you, as a Pastor, to tap into information that otherwise would not be available to you. However, there is a catch. The coach can talk, but more importantly the coach must listen. Too often the literature we read and the lessons we receive on prayer talk about the language of prayer, how we pray, when we pray and what we pray. The real focus of prayer for a pastor, or any Christian for that matter, is not just speaking, but also listening. We are listening for instruction and unction as we seek to lead God‘s people in God‘s direction *by* God‘s direction. It is God telling Abraham to go to a place —I will show you.‖[32]

We are reminded in 1 Thessalonians 5:17 to —pray continually.‖ A pastor‘s prayer does not end with the traditional —amen,‖ only the pastor‘s speaking stops at that point. Just as

---

[29] Richard J. Foster. Streams of Living Water (New York: Harper Collins, 1998), 4.

physical ears cannot be turned off, your spiritual ears ought not either. We are called to forever have our ears open to hearing God's words saying —speak Lord, for your servant is listening.‖[33] Howard Thurman's statement earlier invites us to move from prayer as a —sporadic act‖ to prayer at the —climate of the soul.‖[34] If you see prayer as an activity that only takes place at a given time for a given duration, then you are limiting your understanding of prayer and hindering the very power of prayer itself.

Another spiritual discipline for hearing God's voice, closely akin to prayer, is meditation.

[32] Genesis 22:2

[33] 1 Samuel 3:10

[34] Howard Thurman. *Disciplines of the Spirit*. (Richmond, Indiana: Friends United Press, 1963), 96

Meditation

Meditation is an invaluable discipline for any person. Notice, I did not say any Christian, I said any person. For centuries, Christians and non-Christians alike have found the spiritual fruit of meditation delectable As pastor's we must not only be in touch with God, we must also be in touch with ourselves as we relate to God. Meditation allows us to temporarily remove ourselves from the vicissitudes of life and focus our spiritual eyes upon our soul's insatiable desire to be one with God. The benefits are innumerable. Dwight H. Judy, Professor of Spiritual Formation at Garrett Evangelical Theological Seminary, writes:

> —As we explore the potentials of inner healing through Christian meditation, we are invited by the essential teachings of Jesus as well as the other writings of Scripture to be open to radical possibility. New life does come to us. Minds are changed. Bodies are released from stresses and, in some cases, disease. Hearts are cleansed of hurts and bitterness.‖[30]

18

Dr. Judy intimates a variety of meditative practices including —meditating on God in creation, meditation on Scripture, the Jesus Prayer, and Centering Prayer.‖[31] I encourage you to read more information on all four areas, but I would like to focus on meditation on Scripture. This is something I have personally found very rewarding. Not only is it healthy for spiritual development, but it also lends itself to sermon preparation, which we will discuss in the final section.

Marjorie Thompson sheds more light on this idea of meditating scriptures in a similar discussion as she writes,

> —Spiritual reading is a meditative approach to the written word. It requires unhurried time and an open heart. If the purpose of our reading is to be addressed by God, we will need to practice attentive listening and a willingness to respond to what we hear…the primary focus of spiritual reading for Christians has always been scripture, with good reason. The purpose for which the scriptures were written—presenting hearers with God's word—and the purpose of spiritual reading— allowing ourselves to be addressed by God's Word—are completely consonant. They are as suited to each other as a hand and glove.‖[32]

Both Dwight H. Judy and Marjorie Thompson are strong proponents of *lectio divina* or spiritual reading, and rightly so. —The term came into common usage by the sixth century, when it was used by St. Benedict in formulating the first rule of monastic life,

[30] Dwight H. Judy. *Christian Meditation and Inner Healing* (Akron: OSL Publications, 2000), 5.
[31] Dwight H. Judy. *Christian Meditation and Inner Healing* (Akron: OSL Publications, 2000), 15.
[32] Marjorie J. Thompson. *Soul Feast* (Louisville: Westminster John Knox Press, 1995), 19.
[38] Dwight H. Judy. *Christian Meditation and Inner Healing* (Akron: OSL Publications, 2000), 65.

which became known as the Rule of St. Benedict. From that time onward, the Rule has profoundly shaped Christian life, monastic and nonmonastic alike.[38] Lectio Divina —cooperates with this verbal function of the mind and begins to turn it toward the mystery of deeper dimensions within ourselves.[33] It is divided into four stages:

Lectio	Reading
Meditatio	Meditation
Oratio	Prayer
Contemplatio	Contemplation

Let us use this short piece of text found in Genesis 3:8, as an example and take a quick glimpse at *lectio divina*: —Then the man and his wife heard the sound of the LORD God as he was walking in the garden in the cool of the day.‖

1. *Lectio* is not reading for the sake of covering a specific amount of text. It is not reading with any sort of intentionality at all, other than allowing the words on the page to speak to you. Thompson offers the great analogy of reading a love letter.[34] You allow the depth and weight of every word to have its place and moment in the text. It is a much slower and more deliberate pace than your typical read. It is an expensive wine to be savored not gulped. It is allowing the words to begin penetrating who I am. During this phase, I may read and reread the text in order to position it at the very center of my being.

2. *Meditatio* is quiet listening as we allow those words to marinate in our hearts. It is feeling what the author felt as he wrote the words. It is a quieting time, as my mental

[33] Dwight H. Judy. *Christian Meditation and Inner Healing* (Akron: OSL Publications, 2000), 67.

[34] Marjorie J. Thompson. *Soul Feast* (Louisville: Westminster John Knox Press, 1995), 23.

telescope zooms in on the key thoughts and ideas the words may carry. I am hearing God's footsteps slowly touch the ground in the garden. I smell the garden at a cool time in the day. I am feeling Adam's heart race as he knows God is approaching. I am allowing the text to absorb me into the story itself. I am allowing God

to speak to me specifically through the text. What is God saying to me right now? Does my heart race in anticipation for God?

3. *Oratio* is my response to God through the meditation. Your soul may respond in a number of ways, from crying out to remorseful surrender to praise and thanks. Here we respond to God and acknowledge His word to us. Here we seek God's help in fulfilling the demands of our *meditatio*.

4. *Contemplatio* is the final process of rethinking, reflecting and reminding ourselves as we prepare to enter life in response to the entire experience.

Other Disciplines

Just like prayer, meditation is a great spiritual discipline. It should be evident by now how beneficial this discipline, along with prayer, is with regard to sermon preparation as well. Ultimately, the most important thing is that you find what works for you.

Keeping that in mind, Marjorie Thompson suggests additional ways beyond prayer and meditation in which we can listen and hear from God. She writes, —we can expect to hear God speak to us through writings that are intentionally called God's Word...The Creator also speaks to us through creation...We often hear God's voice through one another...The circumstances of our lives are another medium of God's communication with us.‖[35]

---

[35] Marjorie J. Thompson. *Soul Feast* (Louisville: Westminster John Knox Press, 1995), 33.

Finally, I don't want to under-emphasize or overcomplicate the concept. Sometimes, it is as simple as taking a break. I took five days in Chicago with my family and what a trying, learning, and wonderful experience it was. With the price of gas so high, we decided to go to near-by Chicago and dig up all we could do. We purchased a City-Pass which gave us access to the Field Museum, Shedd Aquarium, Adler Planetarium and Sears Tower. The first day was trying. Not realizing how much older my kids were (16 and 13), we were four in one hotel room and the challenges were many. The first night we bought a game called Outburst. In this game you try to get your teammate to say a word without you saying it. This was the highlight of the trip. We had always been a game playing family, sometimes eating a steak dinner with a Sorry![36] board in the middle of the table. This wonderful spirit of unity was quickly resurrected and our jail-cell like hotel room became the most anticipated place to be at the end of every day. More importantly, it did something for me spiritually. It reminded me of how great God is as I watched my babies become adults. It reminded me of love, sharing and a father's role of protecting his family. It was not about bottom-lines and meeting deadlines; it was just about having fun and being with the one's I love most. And it felt good. God rejuvenated me through this process.

You will be challenged in new ways during your first year. We must avail ourselves to the ever-speaking voice of God and allow it to power us for the journey. Whether it be a quiet whisper on a cold and snowy day, or the thunderous voice of protestors calling for justice, prayer time in our closet or quiet meditation. God is forever speaking and a pastor must be forever listening. When we walk with our ears open to God, though we may not be speaking, we are still praying. If you have not already done so, make prayer a priority in your life immediately. Start that first year with a good spiritual foundation. You will not be able to lead God's people without God's direction, God's help and God's power. Power Up!

---

[36] Sorry! is a registered trademark of Parker Brothers.

Your personal spiritual time is closely attached to how you manage your vocational time, i.e. the time I am at work. In order to enjoy more time away, things must be able to run efficiently without you. People must also understand how beneficial these breaks are for the Pastor and the Congregation; else, it may be misinterpreted as a Pastor who is lazy or does little work. How the church runs can present procedural challenges and how the people think can result in perspective challenges.

Procedural Challenges

Culture Shifts, by Lewis and Cordeiro, talks about understanding the culture of a church and seeking to transform the culture as opposed to trying to change a few people.[37] As I examined my own spiritual life, I began to examine the culture of my church, specifically the spiritual culture. It quickly became apparent to me that my analytical goal-driven personality had translated into ministries and leaders who were of similar suit. Just as I was driven by statistic and objectivity, so were they. If there was going to be room for —a break‖ and spiritual disciplines, operations at the church would need run more efficiently and more effectively. We had a very tedious calendar comprised of small events and everyone attended their own individual events and usually no one else's. I, on the other hand, was expected to make them all. I believed that it would be more effective and resourceful to have fewer events and solicit greater participation at each as organizations supported one another. This would also ease potential calendar conflicts and ease our schedule overall. I knew an Official Board meeting was coming up and this was a golden opportunity to begin turning the tide.

Our meetings have always started with one verse of a song, a scripture and a quick prayer; this meeting would be different. My hope was to bring God back to the center of focus and remind us

---

[37] Robert Lewis and Wayne Cordeiro. *Culture Shift: Transforming Your Church From The Inside Out.* (San Francisco, Jossey-Bass Publishing, 2005).

of our connectedness to God through our ministries. I set aside fifteen minutes for devotion, as opposed to the normal five we were accustomed to spending, and drawing from various resources, I offered the following devotional thought:

Official Board Meeting Devotion Song: Lord Prepare Me

Lord prepare me, to be a sanctuary

Pure and holy, tried and true

With thanksgiving, I'll be a living Sanctuary, Lord for

you!

Prayer: St. Augustine's Prayer for Holiness

Breathe in me, O Holy Spirit, that my thoughts may all be holy. Act in me, O Holy Spirit, that my work, too, may be holy. Draw my heart, O Holy Spirit, that I love but what is holy. Strengthen me, O Holy Spirit, to defend all that is holy. Guard me, then, O Holy Spirit, that I always may be holy. Amen.

Scripture: John 15:1-8 (NIV) *"I am the true vine, and my Father is the gardener. He cuts off every branch in me that bears no fruit, while every branch that does bear fruit he prunes so that it will be even more fruitful. You are already clean because of the word I have spoken to you. Remain in me, and I will remain in you. No branch can bear fruit by itself; it must remain in the vine. Neither can you bear fruit unless you remain in me.*

"I am the vine; you are the branches. If a man remains in me and I in him, he will bear much fruit; apart from me you can do nothing. If anyone does not remain in me, he is like a branch that is thrown away and withers; such branches are picked up, thrown into the fire and burned. If you remain in me and my words remain in you, ask whatever you wish, and it will be given you. This is to my Father's glory, that you bear much fruit, showing yourselves to be my disciples.

Reflective Thoughts:

What fruit is my ministry bearing?

25

What needs pruning?

What could bear fruit, but needs more attention?

Questions to be answered aloud:

The _____ministry is here to provide the church with_____.

This is important to God because_____.

We are doing this by_____.

The results were amazing. There was truly a sweet, sweet spirit in this place. Procedurally, we were moving towards working as one body. I had already heard through the grapevine that a few organizations were concerned about losing their events and others were concerned with not have their own money. Honestly, I was carrying some anxiety over this and, as a spiritual burden, it was slowly gaining weight. I knew the committee had worked hard to come to these conclusions and we knew some of these changes were important for my personal time and spiritual growth as well as unifying the church body. It was decided that many of the small ticket events we were having would be removed from the church calendar and we would focus on those events that yielded the largest revenue. This included many events that had been standing for years.

I believe this devotion placed people in a spiritual place that they could more clearly see that the needs of body superseded the needs of their individual organizations. God had his way! Focusing on God and scripture allowed us to forget ourselves and see the bigger picture, i.e. spiritual disciplines. In addition, we removed twelve events from the next year's calendar, which meant more time for me, i.e. break time. Church procedures directly impact your ability to create room for personal spiritual development. Please note that changing the church calendar is not something I would recommend during the first year, instead, I am hoping to show the connection between how your church operates and your ability to find personal time. As you are learning the *modus operandi* of your new charge, take note of what time space is carved out for you. Again, the first year is very opportune because it's easier to start with the time set aside than it is to force it in once your schedule is full.

Perspective Challenges

We are moving in a direction of empowerment. We are developing leaders to lead and take ownership of their God-given ministry. Culturally, this has been challenging. Many come from the ―old school‖ where you ask the Pastor everything, and I mean everything. What color do you want the toilet paper to be? I have tried to steer away from micro-managing for reasons previously stated, but my appearance of indifference has sometimes been misinterpreted as just that, indifference or not caring. The people needed a change in perspective with regard to our respective roles in the church.

As we began to see our individual organizations as ministries, we had to come to the harsh realization that many of us were not bearing fruit. This is when the ideas of Kenneth Bakken[38] came to mind, as you will see in a moment. I know it is one thing to have a welcoming church, and it's another to have welcoming ministries within the church. Many churches welcome new members as long as they stay in their lane. This is not the healing church that Jesus desires us to be. A long overdue change in perspective needed to take place.

We had some trouble at our July Official Board meeting. As we were planning for the Annual Church Picnic, a young lady in

---

[38] Kenneth L. Bakken. *The Journey into God.* (Minneapolis, Augsburg, 2000).

charge of the young girls Praise Dance Team asked if the young girls could help serve this year. The Kitchen Committee immediately shot the idea down and in a not-so-friendly manner. This bothered me on a number of levels. I called the Kitchen Committee into my office in order to hear their explanation. ―We are a team and the kids just mess up the routine and make it harder for us to do our work.‖ I asked them, ―Who said love was convenient?‖ We conversed a little while longer and they left. It was hard to determine if they really understood my disdain or if they were just accommodating my ideas because the Pastor said so. I preached a sermon that Sunday using Acts 9:10-22 as my text. I talked about Ananias hesitation in going to Saul and how he still called him ―Brother‖ once he got there. We don't determine who comes; we are called to accept whoever God sends. Using ideas from Bakken's book, I spoke about the difference between being ―cured‖ and being ―healed‖ and how we are called to be a healing community where all can come and be accepted, even where we cannot cure. Somewhere between Bakken and the Bible, something took root. I am pleased to say at the next Official Board meeting (August) the Kitchen Committee announced that they had enlisted a number of the young girls to help. A transformation had taken place. We will be carrying Bakken's concept of healing with us.

This perspective change is most paramount as it relates to the mission of our church, but also to my personal time. My kitchen committee had to learn that the picnic was more about people participating and feeling accepted and less about a perfect pile of baked beans. Now, they joke with me about being ―called in the office‖ like a kid in school. A Pastor never wins (smile).

Regarding my personal time, If welcoming ministries become healing ministries that welcome more people, not only will they find joy in satisfying God's purpose, but they will also find their ministry empowered to do more on their own. There are so many people on the picnic serving committee that it is now self-sustaining. Keeping it simple, the more they can do on their own, the less I have to do. Your objective is always self-sustaining ministries that require little personal attention and thus leave more time for personal spiritual development and other necessities. Please don't misunderstand me. I will always be an active Pastor doing my best to insure the success of the church and God's people. A good leader stays informed. But as I stated before, the question has changed and the day is now fresh and new. What's in the best *interest* of the church? Go in with the mindset of empowering your people so you can empower yourself!

Allow me to stress that for you to simply disappear unexplained may not be a smart management move. It is important that not only you, but your congregation also understand the importance of your *sabbath*. It is also imperative that they be able to operate effectively in your absence. They will know not to call or expect quick responses and they will operate in a way that allows this break to flow more naturally and with less friction if they are on board.

Conclusion

There will be challenges to creating spiritually productive space. If you recognize the interconnectedness of your well-being and the health of the church you are coming into your first year with the right thoughts. Procedurally, don't be scared to negotiate your schedule when you enter. This is also the best time to set devotional time as a priority in people's minds. Recognize that how your church operates will greatly impact your spiritual growth and that it is important that they understand your need as much as you do.

Spiritual Disciplines is an area that one could devote their entire life to studying. As you educate yourself on the subject of spiritual disciplines, remember, the key is finding what is most fruitful for you. Then, start NOW! Others, such as myself, may offer suggestions, ideas and methods, but ultimately, our souls and bodies don't always respond the same. Find what works for you! Remember, I mentioned Doug Theisen earlier, you know, the guy with 8,000 members? If anybody can appreciate a spiritual break, I'm sure he can. Listen to his thoughts as my closing remarks on spiritual disciplines and self-care and find what works for you:

—First is to understand how you are uniquely wired and what is it that recharges your batteries. And not to not feel guilty about doing that, because you are not serving your congregation well, if you are not taking care of yourself well. So for me, I love reading a good book, I like listening to podcasts of other preachers when I run in the morning…The one hour a day thing is a great idea, but that might not be ideal for everyone…We have to be a student of ourselves. Especially, if this is your second church there should be some things you know better about yourself…You can't take a cookie cutter approach to spiritual growth. If you aren't a reader then reading is not going to work. Go for audio tapes. We stumbled onto this a few years back. We had people coming to us saying I have never grown more than I have at Heartland. I feel so close to God, I want more. Can you give me more? There is a hunger that comes from starvation, but there is also a hunger that comes from growth, like a 13 year old who won't stop eating. Some people are like that. And we realized that people grow different[ly]. What feeds a mouse would starve an elephant. What feeds an orchid would starve a cactus. How do I grow? I might be less a cactus and more a Lillie but, I need what I need.‖[39]

---

[39] Doug Theisen. Interview by Author. Lead Pastor, Heartland Community Church, Rockford, Illinois, February 8, 2011.

HOW WE PRESENT OURSELVES

Introduction

A wise man once said that first impressions are everything. Well, they are not everything, but they sure do come close. From the moment you meet someone that person is developing and redeveloping a mental file of who you are based on each and every observation the person makes. It is an unfortunate reality that oftentimes people can be so firmly decisive in their first conclusions regarding others that it can be nearly impossible for them to see that individual in any other way in the near future.

As the leader of the church we have to be careful how people see us. As the pastor, all eyes will be on you, even when you don't know it. In our first year, the eyes are even more scrutinizing and the perceptions more important, for these are the perceptions that will undergird your ministry. How we present ourselves in the first year can greatly impact the degree of difficulty or ease with which we lead the people in the years to come.

For this reason, we want to consider carefully how we present ourselves. Unlike corporate American leadership that relies on statistical results as measuring tools of success, clergy must also retain a degree of moral confidence from their constituency. In a world, full of lies, deceit and scandal, people are looking for a human example of Christian growth, not necessarily a finished product, but minimally, a sincere work in progress.

You must know from the very outset that you will not live up to everyone's expectations. If you attempt to please everyone and be everything to everybody, you will ultimately fail. You do, however, have to keep your finger on the pulse of the congregation as a whole so that you are aware when the church is generally displeased.

Misguided Expectations

One of the unique things about a church is that it is one of the few organizations that exist today that is multigenerational. This means that you will have people whose ages range from 8 months to 80 years all in the building at the same time. As times have changed, so has the role and expectations of the Pastor. People have also had different church experiences and different levels of interactions with their pastors. Your congregants will bring a wide variety of expectations to the table and it will be your job to sort and prioritize these expectations. Admittedly, some of these expectations will seem unfair and borderline impossible. These expectations are drawn from their perception of you as a pastor, and oftentimes misconstrued perceptions can lead to misguided expectations.

Dan Reiland, in his book, *Shoulder to Shoulder*,[40] talks about the seven misconceptions about a pastor's life. This list is as follows:

1. Pastors have an easy job.
2. Pastors have a model life.
3. Pastors are experts in their field.
4. Pastors are blessed with ideal marriages.
5. Pastors enjoy the fellowship of many close friends.
6. Pastors consistently experienced a vibrant walk with God.
7. Pastors are content and fulfilled in their work.

The reality is there could be nothing further from the truth. A few of these are probably true for you, and for the rare few who have had the benefit of time and experience, this entire list may be true. However, this list clearly does not exemplify the *normal* life of the average working pastor.
They are misconceptions.

As a result of these misconceptions, people will often bring misguided expectations. For example, because you have an easy

---

[40] Dan Reiland. *Shoulder to Shoulder: Strengthening Your Church by Supporting Your Pastor*. (Nashville, Injoy, 1997), 5-8.

job, you should always be available to me. You don't want to get bogged down trying to live up to unrealistic expectations. This is a defensive approach. As I stated before, trying to please everyone will be a setup for failure and disappointment in both you and them. I, following the offerings of Dan Reiland, am suggesting an offensive approach where you establish and strive for positive balanced expectations of yourself, *for* yourself. Here is a list of realistic expectations, based on the survey responses; we will discuss them one by one:

1. Compassionate
2. Patient
3. Cooperative
4. Impartial
5. Humility
6. Competent
7. Righteous
8. Professional
9. Committed

Expectation 1: COMPASSIONATE – "Rejoice with those that rejoice, mourn with those that mourn."[41]

I surveyed members across a wide array of denominations and church sizes. We asked them: —What first impression do you look for when a new pastor arrives?‖ In our survey, the number one —first impression‖ people look for is how a pastor interacts with the people. 64% of the responses referred, in some way, to how the pastor relates with the congregation. Here are a few excerpts taken from the survey:[42]

—how he/she relates with the new congregation‖ —new pastors should be inviting‖

---

[41] Romans 12:15

[42] Virgil Woods. "Church Member Survey" via www.surveymonkey.com. Jan-Feb 2011.

[49] Bible Study Class, Allen Chapel AMEC, Rockford, Illinois. December 8, 2010.

—how they treat the people they come into contact with‖
—ability to connect with the whole congregation‖
—how he interacts with different age groups‖

People want to know how much you care before they know how much you know. If you have ever had a boss who was a jerk, then you can skip this paragraph because you already know. Seriously, I would contend that if you don't already have an innate desire to love the people, you are probably in the wrong profession.

Our survey reveals that people will be looking for signs of compassion. This is such a key area, that I want to share a short list of these signs with you. This quick list comes from a Bible Study class who was asked, —How do you know when people care?‖ These were the most common responses:[49]

- Listening
- Do you know their name
- Eye contact
- Your presence
- Sacrifice of time
- They prayed for me

Unfortunately, our world can be a very cruel place to live, and because of this, people are constantly looking for compassion. Congregants will appear to have everything in order on the outside and often have hurts hidden deep on the inside. The word —compassion‖ is really a compound word. The prefix —com‖ denotes togetherness as in community. The word passion in its original intent means —suffering‖; thus the crucifixion is often called the —passion‖ of Christ. Compassion is really shared suffering.[43]

---

[43] Based on Random House Dictionary, 2011 via www.dictionary.com. [51]
Philippians 4:6

When I took my son for his first shot, I almost cried myself. I cried because I could see the fear in his face as he sat on the doctor's table. His pain was my pain. It was shared suffering. This is compassion.

People want to know that you care enough that their pains are your pains. We leave jobs everyday where compassion does not exist and bosses do not care. The church cannot be the same. Rejoice with those that rejoice, mourn with those who mourn. Show them compassion! At the end of the day, this is not about numbers, figures, buildings, education wings, programs, ministries, banquets, etc. This is ultimately about people— God's people. We start here because compassion must undergird everything you do.

Expectation 2: PATIENCE – Be Anxious For Nothing[51]

We also asked people, —What do new Pastors do that bothers you? Here are the most common responses:[44]

Make Changes Too Fast	36%
Show Favoritism	25%
Arrogance	14%

It is from these responses that we glean our next four positive expectations.

Meet Bishop John Richard Bryant. He is the Senior Bishop of the African Methodist Episcopal Church. He holds a Doctorate from Colgate Rochester Divinity School and a Master of Theology Degree from Boston University School of Theology. During his 23 years as Bishop, he has signed over 5,000 pastoral appointments spanning from Africa to Los Angeles, from the West Indies to India, from the Caribbean to Nova Scotia and beyond. Even his work prior to elevation speaks volumes. In only thirteen years, he took Bethel AME Church in Baltimore, Maryland, from 500 to over 6,000 members in attendance on Sunday morning. I

---

[44] Virgil Woods. "Church Member Survey" via www.surveymonkey.com. Jan-Feb 2011.

knew his comments would be informed and inspired. I could not wait.

As I sat in his office, I made small chat with his secretary to ease my nervousness. I mentioned the possibility of having him come preach in Rockford and she quickly shared that his calendar was already full over one year in advance. This man's time was precious. In the door walked Bishop Bryant. He was well dressed, as usual, with an African mud cloth vest, subtly denoting pride in his heritage. I followed him in and we began to talk.

Virgil: What is the biggest mistake Pastors make in their first year?

Bishop: The absence of patience. So many tend not to take time to see and discover who they have been sent to. They come in with a passion for what they want, what they want the people to be, what they want the church to be. So they begin to move towards what they want without discovering who the people are.

Virgil: When you come in the door, what should a Pastor's agenda be?

Bishop: The first thing I learned to do was to spend time trying to find out who the people are, what their history is, what their personality is, every church has a personality, just like an individual, what is the personality of that church. While I am doing that, I discovered that the people are more willing to go along with you when the agenda is spiritual. If they don't have a prayer meeting, or bible study, put it in place. It's hard to fight you off of a spiritual agenda--building the spiritual life of the church, building the worship life of the church. You also need to do all you can to introduce yourself to the people; I usually begin by telling them how they can get in touch with me-- where I live, my phone number and that they are free to call me. I also put a resume in the bulletin of who I am as a person, what my life experiences have been like, my childhood, my parents, etc. so that the people can feel that they are getting to know me at the same time I am getting to know who they are.

Virgil: When you first come in, what is most important that the people know about you?

Bishop: That I was excited about being with them. This is also a major mistake that Pastors make. In a system where you are assigned, I found that everybody (parishioners) wants to be wanted; but many pastors, had they had their choice, would not have chosen where they were sent and they make the mistake of communicating that to the people. That's a ditch you have put yourself in. Sometimes, not wanting the post has nothing to do with the people you've been sent to. You may be upset with the Bishop, you may be upset with the Presiding Elder, but these people are watching you as you come through the door and if you send a signal that you don't really want to be here or it wasn't your choice, right away that's a fence or wall that you are going to have to get over.[45]

My conversation with Bishop Bryant clearly reminds us of the need to be patient as we get to know the church and its people. If you ever talk to Bishop Bryant, the first thing you will probably notice is the calm pace of his voice. As he intentionally and strategically weighs his words, he acts as a visible reminder of what being patient looks like.

When you show patience, you will find that it has a calming effect on your congregation. I found early in my ministry, as you will too, that people will take their emotional cues from the leader. When it looks like an emergency to you, it will become an

---

[45] John R. Bryant. Interviewed by author. Chicago, Illinois. February 15, 2011.

emergency to them. When you look confident that a problem will quickly be resolved, the people will be confident as well.

You must remember that this transitional first year will be a time of anxiety for the people--an anxiety that stems from a fear of not knowing what to expect. During this time of relationship nurturing and developing, Bishop Bryant also reminds us of the dangers of sending the wrong first impressions and the importance of understanding the implicit messages that we send, the ones that we may not be aware of at first.

This was a problem area for me for a long time. I am a very high strung, outgoing, Type A personality, as I stated before. New ideas come to me at lightning speed and I'm just a natural —go getter. As a young Pastor, I was excited about the opportunity to prove what I could do and the chance to fix every single problem I saw in the churches in which I have been involved in the past. My youth, energy and idealism were wonderful attributes, but coupled with anxiousness and a lack of patience, they developed in me a sense of frustration.

I had a wonderful Canadian lady, who had been a member of our church for decades. As a matter of fact, three generations of her family had been members of the church going back almost 100 years. She would constantly tell me, —Rome was not built in a day! I would get upset because I felt like she was trying to stifle the growth and direction of the church. Years later, I realized how important these words were.

If you are an impatient person like me (be honest), I want to offer you some very practical advice that has helped me curb this deficiency in my life.

1. Never answer important questions on the spot. Members will try to talk to me or hand me stuff at the most inopportune times, such as standing at the door shaking hands after service. Not only is my mind not in —work mode, but it is very likely I will not remember what we discussed considering the hundreds of people I talk to on a

given Sunday. Having them place this information in my mailbox or e-mailing it, allows me time to revisit the information and make a patient and informed decision. As a caveat, it also shows me that they are serious enough about their idea to put it on paper. So many people have ideas, but very few have the follow through necessary to make them a success.

2. When people stop you in passing, always look them in the eye. Impatient people tend to keep life moving, and unless you are already wandering aimlessly, your members will probably stop you while you are on your way somewhere, with your mind focused on the task at hand. Eye contact says I am stopping and giving this moment to you. Yes, this is often difficult, but not impossible.

3. Pray before you make important decisions. Tell people to give you a moment to pray about it and you will get back to them. Who can argue with a Pastor who wants to talk to God first? As a matter of fact, people will trust your decision making more if they know it is not of you alone. And, you should be talking to God regarding important decisions; after all, this is God's house.

Patience is the key to long-term success. The first year is new and exciting but take a deep breath and relax. You have a long road ahead! Avoid hasty decisions and allow yourself time to marinate on the implications of your actions and allow God a moment to chime in. Patience!

Expectation 3: COOPERATIVE – Let There Be No Divisions Among You[54]

Comments showed that it wasn't the —moving too fast‖ alone that bothered people as much as it was feeling as though they were not consulted or known in the decision making process. Bishop Bryant suggests that we must let the people —get to know us‖ as we —get to know them.‖ Let's go back to our survey and look at a few of the responses that were categorized as Moving Too Fast as it relates to being cooperative:[55]

—It bothers me when a Pastor comes into an existing congregation trying to change policies before consulting with the members.‖
—make a lot of changes without researching if the changes made are necessary‖
—make too many changes without knowing the church‖

---

[54] 1 Corinthians 1:10
[55] Virgil Woods. "Church Member Survey" vi

—make sweeping changes without congregational input‖

Nowhere did the survey suggest that people were not welcome to change. As a matter of fact, I presented this question in the survey: —When a new Pastor arrives, he or she should make changes?‖ Here are the results:[46]

Strongly Disagree	2.8%
Disagree	5.6%
Neither Agree Nor Disagree 63.9%	
Agree	25.0%
Strongly Agree	2.8%

As you can see, it is strongly skewed towards the positive. Pastors should make changes, if necessary, when they arrive. So, it's not the change that is the issue. It is that fact that people want to know that changes are made in conjunction and consultation with the congregation. People want to be heard and feel that their opinions have been taken into consideration.

It is important that people see their pastor as approachable and receptive to information. In talking about our —ideal‖ pastor, the survey returned a number of key words:

- Approachable
- Friendly
- Open
- Inviting
- Listener

I think you get the gist. The warmer and more welcoming you are, especially in the first year, the better off you will be and the easier

---

[46] Virgil Woods. "Church Member Survey" vi
a www.surveymonkey.com. Jan-Feb 2011.

you will begin to develop the relationships necessary for long-term success. These are all signs of cooperation.

However, it does not suffice to simply get to know people. No coach, quarterback, or all-star has ever won a game by themselves. The days of the dictatorial Pastors are slowing fading away, and rightly so. I have found that it is easier to get people to work *with* you than it is to get them to work *for* you. This trend is not unique to the church as most modern literature on leadership is talking more about teamwork and less about being —in charge.‖ I have always thought it arrogant to think I know more than everyone in the group, especially at a church where you have a variety of vocations and levels of expertise. We recently purchased a new facility, and I told my church that if I decorated our church, it would look like a hospital. It would be very clean, very white and very boring. Thank God I have some people who know more than I do, and more importantly, thank God I had the wisdom to team up. Our church is now a wonderful mix of colors that extend beyond my vocabulary of the basic —Crayola 8‖ and much more pleasing to the eye. Show people that you are here to work with them and you are willing to hear what they say. Cooperate!

Expectation 4: IMPARTIAL – There Is Neither Jew Nor Greek, Slave Nor Free…[47]

25% of our respondents said they are bothered most when a Pastor shows favoritism.[48] This was second behind —moves too fast.‖ Most responses spoke to two areas— money and seniority. I will discuss impartiality in general then I will discuss the two specific sub-areas of impartiality individually, i.e. money and seniority.

---

[47] Galatians 3:28
[48] Virgil Woods. "Church Member Survey" vi

It is natural for us, as people, when placed in a crowd, to gravitate towards certain individuals more than others. The reasons for this are numerous, from common interests to curiosity. As pastors, we must be careful in this area, not for the sake of our —favorites‖ but for the sake of others. I do have people with whom I golf regularly and who could probably be labeled as favorites, but I am also willing to golf with anyone in my church. It's an open door. My motto is simple in theory, yet more complex in practice. It is —Do for one, do for all.‖ Anything that I am not willing and/or able to do for everyone, I choose not to do at all. A glimpse of some real-life situations will help provide some clarity.

A good member wanted to have a graduation party at her house. She was well known and I am almost certain no one would have any objection to her borrowing six long tables and some chairs from the fellowship hall for her event. I am also certain that even without it being said, she would return those tables in the pristine condition in which she received them, and had that not been possible, I am also certain that she would have gladly paid for any damages. Clearly, you can see that under normal circumstances this is not a tough decision. That is, unless….you begin to consider the —all.‖ What would happen if members started calling constantly asking for this same favor. We would have to open a rental business in order to accommodate the demands. I had to tell her no, not because I had a problem with it, but because it was not something we were going to be willing to do for everyone.

A wonderful gentleman lost his mother not too long ago. She lived about 3 hours away and I had met her on a couple of occasions. We talked earlier about favorites, well…this gentleman was my golf buddy, a supportive member, and he was also my doctor, as well as my friend.

I wanted to make the trip for the funeral service, but I didn't go. Not because I didn't want to. I didn't go because I wasn't sure how the next member would receive it if the same thing happened and I wasn't willing to make the 6 hour round trip drive for their family member's one hour service. I'm not saying I shouldn't have gone. Sometimes, I still have small questions marks in my head regarding this situation. All I am saying is that —do for one, do for all is a difficult principle to follow.

You always want to think of the long term implications of your actions, particularly with regard to giving an impression of impartiality. Let us look at our survey's two complaint areas in regards to impartiality— money and seniority. Money was clearly the most prevalent comment, so we will focus there and touch upon seniority at the end.

Money

It has been said that romance without finance is a nuisance. I have found that ministry without money can be misery. Not because it can't be done. It's because you feel resourcefully restricted in chasing the vision God has given you. You will need money in order for your church to operate, and lest you forget, envelopes will be delivered to your church every week with these tidy reminders tucked inside called bills. This need often makes showing favoritism towards members who give more money a natural reaction and response.

If your church is very small, it may be that a small group of people have the ability to make or break your financial budget. This is a tough situation because it can potentially lead to power struggles when decisions involving finances are made and, unfortunately, most decisions involve finances in one way or another. By all means, try to avoid conflicts on these terms and/or for these reasons. Here are some thoughts to help you:

Believe God Will Provide

Allen Chapel was started in 1891 and I would always remind my people of that. Why? It says to me that our church was here

44

before any of us got here and that ultimately, God can run God's church without us, even those of us who give the most money AND those of us who preach. The only recourse for a well-giving member is to stop giving. Believe that God's church is bigger than any one person and that God will provide.

This thought process will help you combat the temptation to show favoritism with regards to giving. Yes, we need you, but we won't die without you. This way, you don't feel obligated to acquiesce to expectations based on who gives them and you can operate impartially.

Believe God's People Are Equal

I grew up in a poor family. My mother was a single black woman and she was also physically challenged. I was born when she was 17 years old and my only sister came two years later. We were welfare recipients as my mother made her way through college to become a teacher. She always attended church and loved singing in the choir. My mother would make sure we were in church every Sunday, even if she had to send us on the church bus for Sunday School and meet us there at 11am for service. Some years later, the time came for a new pastor to be elected, as is the tradition in this Baptist church. The discussion ensued regarding who had the right to vote. Many stated that the giving record should be used as an indicator of who was an active member. I don't know what my mother's giving record was, but I knew that we were poor. I remember thinking to myself, this sucks! We don't get to vote for the new pastor.

I share that story because favoritism in this area is personal for me. For this reason, I make a very concerted effort to see all my members as equals. I avoid looking at envelopes or any other indication of individual giving. I do see everyone's giving once a year at tax receipt time, but I try to use this information to see annual trends, not individual donations. The world has enough activities that require money for involvement, church ought not be one of them.

Some people will approach you conscious of their inability to give more, and oftentimes their approaching you is an indication of the guilt they may feel in this area. I tell them they have three choices and ideally they should do them all, if not, do as many as you can. You can write a check, bring a friend, or lend a hand, and, of course, we can pray. The church needs all three. For this reason, I focus on people in all three areas. I have lousy givers who have probably brought dozens of new members to the church and constantly help and participate. I am less likely to be discouraged by them as I am by the person who shows no merit in any of the three areas. Again, I am shifting my focus away from finances alone.

Don't Underestimate God's People

The generations before us grew up during politically volatile times. They witnessed hangings, marches, presidential assassinations, war, disease and more, in the absence of modern technology. I believe this life of uncertainty made them much better than us at one thing, if nothing else—saving money. I don't want to digress into a Dave Ramsey speech, but I do want you to consider this.
Many members, particularly senior members live a very simple and frugal life. Their giving record may not indicate a substantial financial gift, but this does not mean they don't have the capacity.

A senior member came to me and mentioned renovating the kitchen with all new appliances. You must understand, we have a big kitchen. I'm not sure what her giving record was, but I knew that what she was mentioning was bigger than a one person donation, at least, so I thought. Later I realized that she wasn't just asking to renovate the kitchen, she was asking to purchase all of the equipment as well. Never underestimate a member's ability to give. You never know which shell has a pearl, so treat them all equally.

Seniority

Favoritism is a strong word when we talk about working with senior members of our church. What wise leader wouldn't lend an extra ear to those who have been part of the organization the longest? Senior members also tend to have the free time necessary to volunteer during the week, and thus, you will find yourself interacting with them more often. As a result, you will naturally know them better than most.

I literally had to explain to my senior members that on Sunday I am not ignoring them but I am trying to get to know those who I don't see through the week and that it's important that I get to know everyone the same way. More important than my solution is the need to be willing to see the issue. Remain conscious of your impartiality.

Expectation 5: HUMILITY – God Opposes the Proud[49] This third place issue from our survey, arrogance, was not as major, only 14%, but it is definitely worth mentioning and it formulates our fifth expectation--humility. Again, here are some of the responses:

—don't make the officers feel incompetent‖

—being consumed with his self and title‖

—talk about how much they have‖

—be bigger than Jesus‖

I'm sure you don't have to be convinced that no one likes a know-it-all. The only thing more important than knowing what you know is knowing what you don't know. Never try to guess an answer you truly don't know. People will see through your mask. We must remember that we are not God and not be ashamed or so pride-filled that we cannot apologize when we make mistakes or

---

[49] James 4:6

recognize when there are better ideas and ways of doing things than our own. No one expects you to know everything. Free yourself up by giving yourself permission to make mistakes. You will not be the risk-taking leader necessary for success if you are always scared to fail or let someone down. You are the pastor, but you are still human. People will be much more attracted to someone who they know shares their struggles as a human, than someone who is so heavenly bound they are no earthly good.

You should not be arrogant, but you must be confident that the God who called you is going to be there for you. People want to see a confidence that you have in yourself that allows them to put their confidence in you as well. Imagine going in for heart surgery and asking the doctor if he is any good at this and you get this response, "well I'm ok, I just do my best." I'm not sure that's the doctor I want holding my heart in his hand. On the other hand, another doctor may confidently say, "Yes, I am very good at this and I am confident that we will do a good job." Now that's the doctor for me. Just because you believe that you can do a good job does not mean you are suddenly pride filled as long as you remember that all of your wonderful talent comes from God. The pride the Bible warns against is the pride that says —I am better than God‖ or —I don't need God‖ or —I did this myself, not God‖. You *should* be able to say —I am good because God has equipped me for this purpose!‖ That's a healthy pride! People want to see that you are confident in yourself, and more importantly, confident in God. You can't teach what you don't know and you can't lead where you don't go. People need to be confident that you know what you are teaching and you know where you are going.

I am taking the time to make this distinction because our survey showed that people do want a degree of self-confidence in a leader (which could be a tenth unofficial expectation) just not an arrogant leader. Unfortunately, your confidence can often be misread as arrogance so it is important that you understand the difference and delicately balance the two.

Expectation 6: Competent – Study to Show Thyself Approved[60]

As we continue to focus on people's expectations of the Pastor, let us now turn to a different question we asked.

—What part of a Pastor's work is most important to you?‖ The number one response...(drum roll please)....preaching and teaching! 55% of the people surveyed said they see preaching and teaching as the most important part of a

Pastor's work and we will add this as our sixth expectation.

[60] 2 Timothy 2:15

The words were used quite interchangeably in the responses. This suggests that people expect preaching to be informative and teaching to be relative. Preaching should be teaching. We will discuss preaching in much more detail later, but for now, let us focus on the teaching part, particularly teaching God's word. This phrase —teach God's word‖ was very prevalent in their responses.

In lieu of our discussion on arrogance, it is important that you show knowledge in your field of expertise, but in the church, you must do it in a way that does not belittle or demean individuals. Truth be known, some non-degreed members may not have the theological jargon, nonetheless, many are still clearly more insightful theologians than some of the doctors I met in seminary. Don't let your education prevent you from learning from others, but have confidence in your preparation and training.

Competence breeds confidence. We are always more willing to receive information from someone we perceive more knowledgeable than ourselves in a particular area.

I'm not saying come in as the church know-it-all. As I stated, there are many members of my congregation who have been studying the Bible longer than I have been on earth--literally.

However, when I teach, it is very clear and evident that I have taken the time to study, research and prepare for the lesson.

When people ask questions, do not try to make up an answer merely for the sake of having a response. Instead, show a willingness to find the correct answer and bring it to the next class. A good expert not only retains knowledge, but more importantly, knows how to access it. No lawyer would dare memorize the entire law library, but they have to take a course on accessing it because it is the key to their success. You don't have to always have the right answers, just a way to get to them. Even though you don't have the answer on the spot, people will still see you as a source of information and instill confidence in your competence. Finally, remember that some theological questions have no answer, or at least no absolute answer this side of eternity, this is why we discuss and learn together.

Times are changing and one of the expectations being placed on leaders in nearly every field is continuing education. Education is not simply a symbol of acquired knowledge, it's a sign of commitment to your vocation. Education does not guarantee success and lack thereof does not guarantee failure. It does, however, tell people that you have invested time and resources into making yourself a better prepared candidate for this position. I'm not sure I want a lawyer who has never been to law school and I definitely don't want a doctor who hasn't been to medical school. I want my spiritual leader to also be a spiritual learner. This too helps people build confidence in you.

Let us now turn to a different survey question as we round out our list of healthy expectations. When asked —what characterizes your ideal pastor?‖ these were the most common responses (categorized):[50]

---

[50] Virgil Woods. "Church Member Survey" via www.surveymonkey.com. Jan-Feb 2011.

Relationships with the People	25%
Righteous Living	21%
Teaching / Knowledgeable	20%
Humility	9%
Leadership/Professional	8%
Work Ethic	7%

As you can see —Teaching‖ was in a close race for the top. We've discussed two of these already: relationships (compassion) and teaching (competence), let us now move to the other responses to this question and finish our list of positive expectations. Our seventh expectation is righteous living.

Expectation 7: RIGHTEOUS LIVING – Holy and Pleasing to God[51]

Fair or unfair, as the Pastor you will be held to a higher standard of morality and Christianity. People see you as God's representative, more so than the average Christian and expect you to exemplify what a good Christian is.

I don't want to belabor the idea that we all should be striving to live righteous lives. God will be the source of your strength and being as you walk in God's call. Hopefully, the section on Preparing Yourself, has given you a good jump start on Holy living. However, as the Pastor piety takes on a new dimension in your life.

I have a very liberal theology so this area has been challenging. I am a video game fanatic and I love my music loud in my car. Neither of these activities compromises my Christianity in my mind, however, it has been a bitter pill for others to swallow. I don't talk about my video gaming as much as I used to and I

---

[51] Romans 12:1

definitely turn my music down when I pull into the church parking lot. You must be aware of how you are perceived by others and how these perceptions can potentially taint their confidence in you as a Godly leader. It doesn't mean you can't be yourself, it does mean you must be conscious of perceptions.

I was approached by a church member who asked me if it's ok for the pastor to drink liquor. She was shocked by my response, —sure, it's ok, but not in public.‖ I don't find anything wrong with having a glass of wine, particularly in the confines of my home or the presence of my wife or family gatherings. Yet, because I know that this can be a stumbling block for someone else who is looking to me as an example of Christianity, I have chosen to tailor my behavior.

Romans 14:20 says —all food is clean, but it is wrong for a man to eat anything that causes someone else to stumble.‖ NIV

It is often not the activity within itself that's wrong, but how it is perceived by others can cause you to tailor how and when you participate. I believe that some things are best between you and God.

Please don't misunderstand me, if you are doing something displeasing to God, you should stop immediately. Righteous living means righteous living. However, as spiritual leaders, our focus moves beyond our own righteousness into the righteousness of others. We don't want to be stumbling blocks!

Let us now close with a note on the remaining two responses about what people want in a pastor, Professionalism (or leadership) and Commitment (or work ethic). These will comprise our eighth, ninth and final expectations.

Expectation 8: PROFESSIONAL – Let All Things Be Done Decently and In Order[52] People don't just want a leader, they

---

[52] I Corinthians 14:40

want a professional. Timeliness, competence, preparedness, neat appearance, no matter how you dress casual or business, and good follow through build confidence in the people that you are a leader they can follow and depend on.

I have a colleague who was trying to get a project off the ground with the assistance of the Public School system. When I asked one of the school's administrators why they were not signing on, they began to explain to me that this Pastor had forgotten two meetings that he called and was constantly late for the ones he did attend. It was not his Christianity they were questioning, it was his professionalism. Yes, we are pastors, but we are also professionals and must conduct ourselves as such.

Expectation 9: COMMITTED – I Press On Towards the Goal[53]

People also want to see commitment. If it is not important enough for the leader to have a vested interest, then why should I? People's level of commitment will usually never exceed that of the leader. If the leader is always late, eventually the people will be too. As a leader, your level of commitment speaks not only to who you are, but also to the expectations of the people. As a leader, your priorities will eventually become the priorities of your congregants. What are you committed to?

No one likes digging a ditch with a supervisor standing over them unwilling to get his hands dirty. When Moses went into the wilderness, he went with the people.
He didn't ride a chariot, he walked as they walked. When manna came, he ate as they ate. Don't be scared to show up and work side by side with congregants on projects. This sends a very loud message of your commitment to the people.
One of my favorite activities is serving juice during meals. While people are eating, I take a large pitcher of juice and walk around the fellowship hall offering refills. It's a great way to chat

[53] Philippians 3:14

with people, and who doesn't want their juice cup refilled halfway through a meal? And if you are like our church, you probably use those small white cups that only hold two sips anyway. It's not a big gesture, but it shows the people my willingness to work, and I have a great time doing it.

You don't have to do everything around the church all the time, but find some activities that allow you to get your hands dirty. Not only will people love it, but you will find a fresh sense of joy in knowing that you have served in another way.

Conclusion

Starting the race on the right foot means casting the right first impressions and being conscious of the image you are seeking to portray. In all of this, be true to yourself. If you struggle in an area don't be scared to let people know. Casting impressions is a process not a product. It is something you will work on the duration of your career. Our survey returned nine healthy and realistic expectations. As you go into your first year, you want to work at presenting a balanced portrait of these nine traits. Here is that list, one more time:

1. Compassionate
2. Patient
3. Cooperative
4. Impartial
5. Humility
6. Competent
7. Righteous
8. Professional
9. Committed

HOW WE POSITION OURSELVES Introduction

—...When clergy begin their work in a new place, they need to know much more than mere annual reports and orders of worship can tell them. They need to know the congregations stories and its idiom, its ways of feasting and its ways of bestowing honor. The new pastor needs to learn the often unspoken expectations of the insiders and elites, as well as the expectations of those who attend more sporadically. Immediately after a pastor or priest or rabbi comes to a congregation, a careful study of its culture can be invaluable.‖[54] —Culture is the most important social reality in your church. Though invisible to the untrained eye, its power is undeniable. Culture gives color and flavor to everything your church is and does. Like a powerful current running through your church, it can move you inland or take you farther out to sea. It can prevent your church's potential from ever being realized, or—if used by the Holy Spirit—it can draw others in and reproduce healthy spiritual life all along the way.‖[55]

When we talk about understanding the culture of a church, do know that we are opening a Pandora's box that could mean years of projects and study in this regard. I want to offer you some valuable insight into why studying the culture is important, and how you study the culture. My hope is not to generate a project for you to do in the first year, rather, to establish church culture as an ongoing focal point of your leadership, though you may find such a project fruitful later on. As times change, so do cultures.

---

[54] Nancy T. Ammerman, Jackson W. Carroll, Carl S. Dudley, William McKinney. *Studying Congregations: A New Handbook*. (Nashville, Abingdon Press, 1998), 82.
[55] Robert Lewis and Wayne Cordeiro. *Culture Shift: Transforming Your Church From The Inside Out*. (San Francisco, Jossey-Bass Publishing, 2005), 3.

Assessing the culture of your church is an ongoing process. Good assessment prevents assumption. Allow me to share a quick story.

I was raised in a tithing church. I was raised that you don't have chicken dinners and such to raise funds for the church. When I walked into my first church, my mind was already made up that we would become a tithing church. As we met the first few times, we began to develop the calendar for the year and people began to talk about this Game Dinner. Immediately, I was opposed.
—We will not be a chicken dinner restaurant, we are a church!‖ Mr. Jetter was 6' 5‖, 300lbs and constantly wore overalls. Ironically, he was as gentle as a teddy bear. Nonetheless, as Head Steward of the church, when Mr. Jetter spoke, you listened. He pulled me to the side after the meeting and explained to me that this was a 27-year tradition in the community. All of the meat was donated by hunters and fishers in the region and included venison sausage, raccoon, rabbit, squirrel, buffalo meat, frog legs…you get my drift (good rural Iowa food). He began to tell me that the town's politicians would be there and other prominent figures in the community. Of course, I conceded and we had one every year I was there.

Had I taken the time to ask a few questions, get a little more information and see this event in its —cultural‖ context, I would have saved myself some serious headache. Many of your decisions will be much more impacting than a Game Dinner, but it's important that any decision you make takes into account the cultural makeup of the church.

Assessing the culture

When we talk about the culture of a church, we are not simply looking at demographic data. What race are they? What income bracket are they in? How big is the town or city? All of this is important information and does influence the culture of a church, however, culture is a much wider arena than this. Culture reaches into how people think, behave and operate. Culture reaches into how people make decisions. Culture reaches into the symbols on the wall and the smell in the air. Culture is not static but ever evolving. Culture is the uniqueness of a given group of people that make them who they are and determines how they behave.

Eric H. F. Law, author of *Sacred Acts, Holy Change*, employs the very popular metaphor of an iceberg when looking at the culture of a church. On the surface only a small percentage of an iceberg can be seen, while under the surface, the majority of the iceberg is hidden to the eye. It is the larger portion of the iceberg below the surface that is so dangerous to ships because it cannot be seen and thus its size is often underestimated.[56] —In the organizational culture of the church, the part above the water—external culture— includes the appearance of the physical buildings of the church, our worship proceedings, our music, our doctrine…and so on.‖[57] —We must look at the internal culture, the part of the organization's iceberg that is below the water. —These are beliefs and values that we have implicitly learned…They are patterns in our lives we have accepted as normal.‖[58]

We have already begun some of the cultural assessment in the first section of the book, *Getting Started Before The Race*. Obviously, the circumstance offered only a partial view and was more to get our strategic juices flowing. Now we are on site. Every encounter and every experience is an opportunity to learn about your constituency.

Meet Kenneth Copeland. He is the Senior Pastor of New Zion Baptist Church in Rockford, Illinois. He is a gifted musician, wonderful orator and holds a Jurisdoctorate Degree as well as a Master of Divinity. He is the community's resident clergy lawyer. We talked about assessing the culture of the church and he shared these thoughts with me:

---

[56] Eric. H. F. Law. *Sacred Acts, Holy Change*. (Danvers, Chalice Press, 2002), 36.

[57] Eric. H. F. Law. *Sacred Acts, Holy Change*. (Danvers, Chalice Press, 2002), 37.

[58] Eric. H. F. Law. *Sacred Acts, Holy Change*. (Danvers, Chalice Press, 2002), 40.

―A new pastor has to go in with the mindset of a missionary going into a foreign country, the language, how they interact, in some cultures personal space is an issue. For example, I mistakenly hugged a chief member because of the culture I came out of, I miscued doing something counter cultural and the member let me know. I miscued another time, when I had a robe on but no shirt and tie under it, this was important to them. They really tried to make a big deal out of it.

I asked everyone, who wanted to, to come in and spend 45 minutes telling me their personal family story. It took me some months. About 85% took advantage of this. I had no agenda, I just said tell me how you got here and tell me your story. I had a lot of Chrysler employees which gave me a clue to the work ethic of the people. When I started coming in everyday at 6:00am, it made a difference because the men here were factory workers who placed a strong emphasis on hard work. I have an apron of my own in the kitchen, and when I put it on, they look at me and say he is one of us.

We play spades (card game) at my church. So now, in New Members class, everyone has to learn how to play spades. If it's not a sin, why work against it, use it to your advantage.

I gave a survey: What does this church do best? What do you miss most about the old Zion? What are you afraid of as we make this transition?
Everyone said in unison, ―meet and eat!‖ So I took that and ran with it, let's take what you do and fold that into what we are trying to get to.‖[59]

[59] Kenneth Copeland. Interviewed by author. Rockford, Illinois. February 3, 2011. [71]
Robert Lewis and Wayne Cordeiro. *Culture Shift: Transforming Your Church From The Inside Out*. (San Francisco, Jossey-Bass Publishing, 2005), 48.

Understanding the culture of your congregation is paramount to your success. The best pastors, leaders, politicians, CEOs and Presidents are the ones who have a clear understanding of the culture they operate in and are constantly observing for cultural shifts and changes along the way.

Lewis and Cordiero's book *Culture Shift* suggests four areas to look at:

1. *Leadership and values.* What values do members of your church's leadership communicate by their lifestyle?
2. *Vision Statement.* Is your church's vision something people can identify with and use to measure their spiritual lives?
3. *Symbols, ceremonies, celebrations.* The things you honor, remember, and cheer for are the things you most value.
4. *You as leader.* Ask yourself, —What do I want to accomplish here at this church?‖[71]

This is a good starting place and will offer a peripheral view of your church's culture. For a more in depth study, I recommend Nancy Ammerman's book *Studying Congregations.* In a section titled —Methods for Studying Cultures‖, Ammerman offers three focal points to which we now turn: activities, artifacts, and accounts.[60]

Activities

What we do says a lot about who we are. By observing the rituals of a church, we can begin to understand much about how they see

[60] Nancy T. Ammerman and Jackson W. Carroll, Carl S. Dudley, William McKinney. *Studying Congregations: A New Handbook.* (Nashville, Abingdon Press, 1998), 84. [73] Nancy T. Ammerman and Jackson W. Carroll, Carl S. Dudley, William McKinney. *Studying Congregations: A New Handbook.* (Nashville, Abingdon Press, 1998), 84.

God, see themselves and how they see the role of the church. The main ritual that is common to most, if not all, churches is the worship experience. Ammerman calls it —the most intentional presentation of who they are.‖[73] As you observe the worship experience, open all five of your senses. Look beyond what you can see and hear. Smell the air, feel the pews underneath you, observe the banners on the wall, absorb the atmosphere in its entirety. Every small detail contributes in some way to the worship experience. As you observe, look for prevailing themes, what is most important to them?

Music is another key area. Notice the tempo of the music being sung. Are people actively participating in congregational hymns or do they quietly hold their hymnals waiting for the song to end? The volume of the music is important. You may notice that music is considered an afterthought during worship, while in other churches, music is the main attraction. What instruments are being played? How many paid musicians are there? Most churches put their money in places they deem a priority.

Notice the time of the worship. Does the attendance at early morning service look greater than that of late morning service? Does the service seemed rushed as though people are just going through the motions? During my interviews, one pastor suggested looking at how the people operate *after* the worship service. Do people immediately leave the building as though the movie is over or do they stay, mingle, laugh and fellowship as though they are glad to be together again?

Another area to examine is educational activities. Churches teach what they feel is most important. Sitting quietly in the back of a few Sunday School classes can prove very insightful. Sunday School classes often operate as social groups as well. Do they celebrate birthdays during Sunday School? Is there more going on in class than the rigors of teaching and curriculum?

Potlucks, the church picnic and the annual bowling outing are examples of social activities that speak to the culture of your church also. Remember Pastor Copeland? His church loves to play cards; he embraced that and made it a continuing part of the culture. Any time the people gather, for any reason, it is an opportunity to learn about the culture of the church as you observe their participation, or lack thereof.

Artifacts

When archaeologist discover a settlement, it is amazing how much they can discern regarding the everyday lives of a community based on artifacts alone. Scrolls, dishes, tools, and utensils all speak to the general *modus operandi* of a group of people. The church is no different.

The churches main artifact is the building. Is the parking lot clean? Is it fenced in? Is the nursery immaculate or does it look like an afterthought? How is the building space being used? Is it cluttered? What activities have they allocated the majority of space to: youth, games, worship, teaching? Ammerman says, —As you tour buildings, watch for the spaces that are unused, as well as those that are busy.‖[61] Are there certain spaces or areas that are off limits to most? This will speak to what the church sanctifies and holds in high regard.

When observing artifacts, take particular note of the artifacts that the congregation holds out front more than others. What pictures are *prominently* displayed? What furniture occupies the pulpit area? Allen Chapel had something my previous churches didn't have. They had a trophy case. As I read the trophies, I noticed that there was a time when volleyball and basketball were major activities at our church. I also noticed that they were winners of the —Silver Chalice Health Challenge‖ five years in a row. This

---

[61] Nancy T. Ammerman and Jackson W. Carroll, Carl S. Dudley, William McKinney. *Studying Congregations: A New Handbook*. (Nashville, Abingdon Press, 1998), 92.

is a community event where churches receive points by having people participate in blood drives, blood pressure screenings, HIV tests and other health related activities. The artifacts in your church can often tell you what is important to your church.

What is in the pew? If the only thing in the pew is offering envelopes, no bibles, no hymnals, then that is saying something. What version of the bible is in the pew?

Many churches are much more accustomed to the King James Version than more modern translations such as the New International Version or New Revised Standard Version. Are there visitor cards in the pew? If not, what does this say about hospitality and the desire to welcome newcomers?

Accounts

―Listening for how people talk to each other is critical to understanding their culture.‖[62] I always find this part fascinating. What people say to each other? How they say it? How they address each other? I grew up in a church where everyone was Brother So and So and Sister So and So. It subtly reminded us of our relationship to one another as it relates to our common Father. Allen Chapel is much different. Here, we address everyone by their first name, with the exception of the elders of the church. Most of my church is related to one another, biologically, and this use of first names, for them, insinuates a familial degree of comfort with one another. On a more practical note, because they are family, there are a lot of people sharing the same last name. So, if I were to say Sis. Stanford, I know of at least ten to twelve women (no joke) who all may respond to that title. I also noticed that the pastor is always ―Pastor;‖ there is never use of the first name. This shows their high regard for this office in the church. The language they use not only says something about how they see each other, but how they understand the hierarchy of the church.

---

[62] Nancy T. Ammerman and Jackson W. Carroll, Carl S. Dudley, William McKinney. *Studying Congregations: A New Handbook*. (Nashville, Abingdon Press, 1998), 94.

You will also notice that certain individual's vocational titles carry over into the church. We are proud to have Rockford's first African-American Mayor as a member and though his tenure ended years ago, he is still Mayor Box. Doctors are often still referred to as —doctor‖ in the church. Attorneys are often still referred to as —attorney‖ in the church. This says that our congregation's culture is not a closed fence, rather it is influenced by the community at large. What happens out there affects how people see each other in here.

I didn't get to ask this question during our survey, but experience allows me to say be prepared to be called by your predecessor's name. It's natural for people to do this as old habits are hard to break. More importantly, recognize when they do say his or her name, and take note of what conversations invoke this. Pastor J.W. was the Pastor of Allen Chapel three pastors ago. Yet, he is often cited by elder members during Bible Study class. It didn't take long to see the lasting impact this great Pastor had on his congregation and the culture of the church. As a result of his great teaching, it is no surprise that Allen Chapel is posited as a place you come to learn. Understand the history and you can better understand the present.

Accounts also means getting to hear the stories of old. We must listen for *whispering legacies* in our church.[63] I highly recommend a Harvard Business Review Press Book titled *The First 90 Days*, particularly a section called Diagnosing the Business Situation.[64] The author, Michael Watkins, states, —the four broad types of business situations that new leaders must contend with are start-up, turnaround, realignment, and sustaining success.‖[65] He continues,

---

[63] Will Mancini. *Church Unique*. (San Francisco, Jossey-Bass, 2008), 77.
[64] Michael Watkins. *The First 90 Days*. (Boston, Harvard Business School Publishing, 2003), 61.
[65] Michael Watkins. *The First 90 Days*. (Boston, Harvard Business School Publishing, 2003), 61.

—In a *start-up* you are charged with assembling the capabilities (people, funding, and technology) to get a new business, product, or project off the ground. In a *turnaround* you take a unit or group that is recognized to be in trouble and work to get it back on track...In *realignment*, your challenge is to revitalize the unit, product, process, or project that is drifting into trouble. In a *sustaining-success* situation, you are shouldering responsibility for preserving the vitality of a successful organization and taking it to the next level.[66]

If you are dealing with a group of people who have enjoyed a recent era of healthy church growth, they may be more eager to return to those good ol' times. They will operate in a spirit of expectation knowing what a thriving church looks and feels like. If your congregation has been stagnant for an extended period of time, it may be more difficult for them to envision themselves as a thriving congregation. Taking the time to understand the history of your church will afford you the opportunity to more clearly assess your current business situation and will help you tailor your approach toward effective church growth.

Warning! Talk about the Pastors of the past, but never in a negative way. Remember, regardless of what kind of job *you* think they did, you were not here so you don't know. Try to avoid addressing touchy areas if they exist. Look for the strengths in each predecessor's leadership style. I laugh sometimes and say to myself, I wish I had a little George Moore (my immediate predecessor) in me.

After about a year I noticed something odd in the language (accounts) at Allen Chapel. I noticed that every vote we cast was unanimous. No one was disagreeing. It was general practice that you did not oppose the Pastor or presenter in a meeting. I knew

---

[66] Michael Watkins. *The First 90 Days*. (Boston, Harvard Business School Publishing, 2003), 62.

this was not good. I'm pretty cocky on certain days (Lord, forgive me!), but to think that *every* idea I brought was a good idea...that's a little far stretched for me. No healthy organization runs completely off of the thoughts of one mind; we needed input. After some explanation...well, let's just say my meetings became very interesting. More importantly, healthy dialogue and discussion began to take place where it had not before. It wasn't that they did not have ideas, it was that the culture was preventing those ideas from coming forward. I had to change the culture of the meeting in order to get the results I needed. To say the least, I have had some pretty heated discussions and debates, which, according to Patrick Lencioni's book *Death by Meeting*, is a good thing. I have had very irate members stand and passionately express their discontentment in meetings, but I implore everyone to quietly listen, because every member has a right to be heard, as long as no member is disrespected. Again, the language is closely attached to the culture of the church. How we address each other, what we will or will not say, and how we say it, all expresses a deeper understanding of how your congregation sees itself.

The church is like a hospital where sick people get well. The church is like a gym where we build our spiritual muscles. The church is like a lighthouse shining the light of Christ to those who are lost. Accounts also consist of metaphors we use when describing our church and they speak to the culture of the church. Some churches are very mission driven, sending groups out into the streets and across the globe. Other churches are education driven, offering a wide variety of Bible classes and learning opportunities. The metaphors speak to what kind of church we are and what we see as our primary mission.

Open your ears to the people of your church. What is your church talking about?

Conclusion

Understanding the culture of your church is an ongoing process. I still laugh sometimes because I am from Iowa and many of my constituents are from the South. This brings a basket of cultural differences all by itself.

Learning the culture is never going to be cut and dry, it is a judgment call. Don't feel bad when you make a mistake, just be forever learning. Understanding the culture of your church is the most important task. Without it, everything else will inevitably fall short.

It took me three funerals to figure out what I was doing wrong in regards to the culture around bereavement. When a member passed away, the family gathered at the member's house as was the tradition. I called the family, extended my condolences and asked if there was anything they would like me to do. They would say they were fine and thanks for calling. Later, I heard that many were disappointed because the pastor did not visit. In my mind, it was a time for family to gather, and because this was a particularly large family, I knew no one was alone. I asked if there was anything I could do and all they had to say was please stop by, but they didn't. I saw my potential visit as an intrusion on their private time unless I was invited. So, again, in *my* mind, I did what I was supposed to do. This happened again and coincidentally it was another large family. I played my same hand and received the same result. I asked my secretary, Sis. Stanford (yes, that's her name) about it, because I knew she was indigenous. She explained to me that no one was ever going to ask me to come by. Culturally, it was a given expectation, one that I obviously was unaware of, that the Pastor visits the bereaved family. Now, as best as my schedule affords me, I show up, yes, even uninvited. Seems crazy to some of you reading this, but let me assure you, I have never felt unwelcome, at least not in this culture.

I close with this story because it is important that you know some decisions are not a matter of right or wrong. In my social context, my choice would have been correct. In this social context, it was incorrect. Right or wrong is not a matter of individual decision making, it must take into account the culture in which it is executed. This is why understanding the culture is so important.

How We Promote Ourselves

Introduction

I write this as the closing section for a number of reasons. First, growing your church doesn't start with the church, it starts with you; thus the previous sections of this book. Secondly, this is not a book about church growth, at least not directly. There is no magic wand, or hidden formula, for growing your church, as I learned and you will too. Rick Warren offers valuable insight when he begins to discuss the difference between growing your church and allowing your church to grow. He contends, and I agree, that the question to ask is not —how do I grow my church,‖ rather, —what is keeping our church from growing?‖[67] This leads to my final section. I wanted to leave you with these thoughts so that as you navigate through your first year of the church, you can think deeply in the area of Hospitality. It's not that Hospitality will grow your church, it's that a lack thereof will definitely prevent your church from growing. There is nothing worse than coming into a church with great preaching, an awesome pastor, inspirational music and wonderful ministries, only to find a group of nonwelcoming cantankerous people.

What is hospitality?

I have had the wonderful experience of serving three churches in two countries in three different social settings. My first church was Bethel AME Church in rural Clinton, Iowa. In two years, our membership grew from 35 to just short of 100. My second church was Grant AME Church, Toronto, Ontario, Canada, located in the fourth largest city on the continent. In two years, our membership grew from 150 to over 300. The church I currently serve, Allen Chapel AME Church is located in the mid-size

---

[67] Rick Warren. *The Purpose Driven Church*. (Grand Rapids, Zondervan, 1995), 15.

68

Midwestern city of Rockford, Illinois. In my first three years here, our membership has grown from 65 to over 250 and now is over 400. As I write, we are preparing to celebrate 5 years in our new 32,000 square foot facility. Though none of my congregations are considered large or mega churches, they have afforded me a unique opportunity to assess church growth in multiple social contexts. Every church I have served, I asked the new members why they chose to join our church. My ego wants to hear them say how informative and impacting my preaching is or how moving the music and the choir are. Contrary to common belief, that was never the answer. They were important in keeping people there, but they were never the main attraction. In every setting and every city the answer has remained the same—I felt loved and I felt welcomed. I consider these answers the bench marks of genuine hospitality.

Consider some of the following definitions of hospitality:

> the friendly reception and treatment of guests or strangers.[68]
> – Random House

> Hospitality offered by a congregation surely includes attention to extending invitations, offering convenient parking places, providing a friendly welcome, and giving clear information about how to navigate the facility and programs. But at its core, Christian hospitality comes from a deep spiritual well and is profound, illuminating, and primitive. It is about bearing witness to the saving love of God.[69] – Neil M. Alexander, President and
> Publisher of the United Methodist Publishing House

> Christian Hospitality is the active desire to invite, welcome, receive, and care for those who are strangers so that they find a spiritual home and discover for themselves the

---

[68] hospitality. Dictionary.com. *Dictionary.com Unabridged*. Random House, Inc. http://dictionary.reference.com/browse/hospitality (accessed: March 17, 2011).

[69] Neil M. Alexander. *CircuitRider*. V.33 No.1. Nashville: Cokesbury, 2008.

unending richness of life in Christ.[70] – Bishop Robert Schnase, author of *The Five Practices of Fruitful Congregations*.

Hospitality is not to change people, but to offer them space where change can take place.[71] – Henri Nouwen, Catholic Writer

You will notice from the above definitions that for the Christian, hospitality has a deeper meaning than that of a welcoming environment. It is an expression and extension of the love of Christ felt in us all as God welcomed us into his/her house. Yes, greeters, ushers, and welcome kits are key components of extending hospitality, but more important is the lasting expression of heart-felt warmth experienced by those who are being welcomed. It is not another program designed to increase church membership; it is a response to the mandate of Christ to let our light so shine into the world. Diana Butler Bass, in her book *Christianity for the Rest of Us*, writes, —True Christian hospitality is not a recruitment strategy designed to manipulate strangers into church membership. Rather, it is a central practice of the Christian faith—something Christians are called to do for the sake of that thing itself.‖[72]

Genuine hospitality must reach all people and this is where most churches fall short. We have an easy time inviting those who most look like us, but we fail to recognize the others we encounter every day at the grocery store, the bank, the school and the gas station. Our church printed thousands of invite cards that we asked all the members to carry and hand out. When I asked my predominantly African-American church how many invite cards they had given to non-black people, the answer was few to none. This quick assessment led me to move our church in a new direction regarding hospitality.

[70] Robert Schnase. *Five Practices of Fruitful Congregations*. Abingdon Press, 2007.

[71] Henri Nouwen. *Reaching Out*. (New York, DoubleDay Press, 1975), 51.

[72] Diana Butler Bass. Christianity For The Rest of Us. (SanFrancisco, Harper, 2006), 81.

When we look at the word —hospitality‖ it is important to know that one of its Latin root word is *hostis*, which means stranger, but it also means enemy, i.e. someone who is *hostile*.[73] We are called to invite our friends *and* our so-called enemies. Hospitality has traditionally been defined as the welcoming of strangers, but the hostel part has generally been omitted. Hospitality can be a scary thing, particularly when dealing with people who don't look, think or smell like you do. Genuine Hospitality must walk in the love of Christ that overcomes this fear and sees the greater need to take that love of Christ to all people; even the ones we don't care for and yes, even the ones who are hostile.

When we look at our churches, we must consider hospitality on three levels.

1. To The Church – How are we encouraging people to visit our church?

2. At The Church – How welcome do people feel when they do visit our church?

3. In The Church – Once a part of the church, do they feel a true sense of belonging?

To The Church

When we talk about genuine hospitality and the ability to attract all people to our church, the first thing we must look at are the mediums that we use to reach into the community and attract people to our church.

Where we advertise says a lot about who we are trying to attract. If the only place you position business cards and posters is

---

[73] "hospitality." *Online Etymology Dictionary*. Douglas Harper, Historian. 17 Mar. 2011. Dictionary.com http://dictionary.reference.com/browse/hospitality

the local High Schools, you inevitably will be drawing on a High School crowd. If you only place advertisements in Nursing Homes, you inevitably will draw on a senior crowd. It is important that we strategically advertise in places that can be seen by all walks of life. Some good places are grocery stores, shopping malls, libraries and other public places. These places generally enjoy a wide range of cultures as their constituents and thus expose your church to a wide range of people.

What our advertising looks like also says a lot. The first thing people look for when they enter a room is those who most closely resemble themselves. As an AfricanAmerican, I generally, even subconsciously, walk into a room and immediately notice how many other AfricanAmerican males there are. There is a general human tendency to look for ourselves in a crowd. This tendency also relates to advertising. Your church website should show images of all ages and all ethnicities if you are trying to attract all people. Likewise, your church brochure and any other print advertising should do the same. Our church had one white person when I arrived and no website. When we built our first website, I intentionally included images of Caucasians, Hispanics and Asians to show our concern for all. We now have more Caucasian people joining and a Hispanic family who recently joined as well. It's a start.

At The Church

First impressions are everything (remember?). This proverbial business saying also rings true with regard to hospitality. Mark Waltz, Pastor of Grace United Methodist Church in Granger, Indiana writes, —The first impression occurs before the service begins—before the reading of the Scripture, before a song is sung, before the message is spoken. First impressions happen in the parking lot, at the entry of your building, in the children's hallways, and in your lobby or narthex.‖[74]

72

Our doctoral student group visited Quinn Chapel AME Church in the downtown Chicago area. It is a thriving predominantly black church located in a predominantly black neighborhood. One of our professors, a white lady, arrived a little late and asked a young black man which door she should go in. He walked her to the door, opened it for her and told her —welcome.‖ She shared this story with us as she expressed how sincere this gesture felt. The typical person would have pointed at the door or instructed her to the door, but this person went the extra mile. Did I mention this was in the middle of a Chicago January snowstorm? This first impression meant a lot.

It is important that our members understand that hospitality starts in the parking lot with them. Too often hospitality is relegated to a committee of Greeters, Ushers or such and it is pushed off as *their* job. As people scurry across the parking lot they should be speaking to one another. They should ask those they recognize as visitors if they have been here before. This creates the welcoming atmosphere before you enter the building.

Speaking of which door to enter, it is also important that guests be able to navigate the property easily. One of the challenges we have had at Allen Chapel is getting people to recognize which of the four entrances leads to the sanctuary. We are in the process of rectifying this. Greeters should not only greet people, but they should direct them to the Sanctuary, coat racks and restrooms when necessary. It is always a strange feeling to be in a foreign place, and our job is to minimize that feeling as much as possible.

There are also ways to make your worship experience hospitable. We recently experimented with digital media by sharing the liturgy and songs on a screen for all to see. The result was amazing. Guests commented on how much easier it was to follow the flow of the service and, as a bonus, I was surprised at how

[74] Mark Waltz. *CircuitRider*. V.33 No.1. Nashville: Cokesbury, 2008

many long standing members said they never knew all the words to some of the liturgy. Remember, the idea is to make a person feel comfortable and at home. Eileen D. Crowley writes in her book *Liturgical Art for a Media Culture*, —For individual members of a congregation, the inclusion of media in worship can mean greater access to the worship experience itself. It can be a mark of hospitality.‖ She also reminds us to be conscious of the images that we are using. —Diversity in the imagery of peoples, places, genders, and ages should be a consistent goal of media ministry.‖[75]

C. Michael Hawn, a faculty member at Perkins School of Theology, offers a four-tier understanding of worship. First, there is the culturally uniform worship. This assumes that the participants have a common background and way of viewing the world. Second, there is worship through cultural assimilation. —This practice assumes a dominant cultural perspective that will become the common currency for all participants…‖ Third is the culturally open worship. This type of worship will —display a spirit of receptivity toward the community's cultural diversity, even though the congregation has a distinct cultural majority group.‖ Fourth is a cultural partnership. —A cultural partnership takes place when no clear majority dominates and culturally diverse members reflect on the surrounding neighborhood and work together in a shared Christian community.‖[76] It is this fourth tier that is hardest to achieve, yet most ideal if our worship is to be truly hospitable.

I had the wonderful opportunity to share in worship with a reconciling United Methodist Church on the West Side of Chicago.

---

[75] Eileen Crowley. *Liturgical Art for a Media Culture*. Collegeville, MN: Liturgical Press, 2007.

[76] C. Michael Hawn. *One Bread, One Body: Exploring Cultural Diversity in Worship*. (Bethesda, MD: Alban Institute, 2003).

As a pastor, it was a good reminder of what it felt like to be the guest. Because I am AfricanAmerican, I was sincerely curious as to how welcoming the worship experience would be. I was greeted pleasantly at the door and welcomed by a number of people. This was a good start. They had a projector screen that helped me follow the service, this was a better start. Then came the straw that broke the camel's back. I saw on the program —Pass Me Not‖, a traditional African-American hymn, and I was a little excited. When the time came to sing the hymn, what happened was even more amazing. They did not use the traditional melody of the song; they actually sang the modern gospel remix to the song. Here I was, in a predominantly white reconciling United Methodist Church, and I was getting my praise on! As if that were not enough, we closed the service with a very traditional song of the Black Church, —I Thank You Jesus.‖ I applaud this pastor because it was clear that their worship experience was constructed with a little something for everyone. This is what a cultural partnership looks like and it is genuine hospitality at its best!

If our worship experience is going to be a cultural partnership, then we must develop our programs with a high degree of intentionality when it comes to including others. Not only did I enjoy the songs of my tradition, but I also enjoyed the rock and revolution songs that I was being exposed to. Because there was something in it that made me feel at home, I was in a better place to receive that which was new and foreign to me. In essence, in its totality, this combination made the worship feel not so foreign at all.

In the Church

So you have loved them in the parking lot, you have greeted them in the door, you have comforted them in the worship service and they have joined church—now what? This is where the true test of genuine hospitality lies. The story is told of a church that was renting its building to a Hispanic congregation. They were loved and welcomed with open arms, until it came to the trustee meetings.

A sense of frustration set it when they were allowed to rent the building, but not be a part of the decision-making process. The attitude, more plainly put, was —it's ok to drive on our road as long as you stay in your lane.‖ When members join our church, I constantly remind them that we have no hierarchy built on seniority. I do this because many new people are not encouraged to take leadership positions in the church; they are told to stay in their lane. A genuinely hospitable church is one that encourages full participation of its members, new and old.

These new members are also a vital resource in assessing just how hospitable your church really is. Please read this closely…**hospitality can never be critiqued by those extending it, only those receiving it.** As an African-American I have met a number of great Christians who extended the utmost heart-felt hospitality and did not realize that some of what they were doing was offensive to my culture. It was not that they didn't care, they just didn't know.

It was a hot summer day as hundreds of people gathered in the park for our neighborhood ice cream social. The other prominent church in our neighborhood is a predominantly white Lutheran church with about 1,500 members. As their pastor called me to the stage, he closed by saying —I know him personally, he's a good boy.‖ If you could have seen the look on my congregation's face. Apparently, someone explained this to him as I received a phone call apologizing the next day. I knew it was an act of ignorance, not malice and I assured him I was ok. We laughed about it and have been fine ever since.

Conclusion

Do not assume that just because you love God and have the best of intentions that your hospitality may not have nuances that may be offensive to certain cultures and people. Allen Chapel has enjoyed a few Caucasian people joining in the last year. Our next step is to take them to lunch and ask them what we can do to be more hospitable to their culture. Again, hospitality is something that you have to work at. It requires strong strategic and intentional thought and planning. It is important that what we say with our mouths and hearts is echoed in what people experience.

As a final thought, I have considered asking some of my friends to attend our church as secret customer service assessors. Restaurants have been using this concept for years. This may be a way for us to recognize areas where change and growth is needed. Genuine hospitality is not a goal, it is a journey. It is a journey that requires time and patience. We live in an ever changing world and we must constantly assess how we are meeting the needs of the people around us. If you are serious about growing your church, genuine hospitality must be in place. They will know that you are his disciples (not by the preaching or singing but…) by the love you show one another.

How We Preach

Introduction

I asked the following questions in our church member survey and here are the top three responses:

What part of a Pastor's work is most important to you?[77]

Preaching and Teaching	55%
Meeting Needs	14%
Spiritual Growth	10%

What do you think the Pastor's primary task should be?[78]

Preaching and Teaching	40%
Spiritual Growth	26%
Meeting Needs	19%

I have pastored long enough to know that many pastors have grown healthy sustainable ministries on a wide variety of gifts. Some pastors are natural administrators, some are natural nurturers, some are natural preachers, and some are natural leaders and organizers. We all bring different gifts to the table. Preaching may or may not be your forte, but according to our survey, it is a substantial part of people's expectations and it is something you will need to work on and work at, regardless of your inherent skill in this area. Remember, the Bible elevates the importance of

---

[77] Virgil Woods. "Church Member Survey" via www.surveymonkey.com. Jan-Feb 2011.
[78] Virgil Woods. "Church Member Survey" via www.surveymonkey.com. Jan-Feb 2011.

preaching even higher by reminding us that [79]it is the foolishness of preaching by which people are saved.[92]

Find The Time

Much of the recent emphasis on preaching is the result of media portrayals of worship service we find on television. It is rare that a television ministry will broadcast all aspects of the worship service, i.e. the prayer, scripture or benediction. I did a quick side study[80] and randomly watched a few dozen television broadcasts and found that over 90% of their airtime was given to broadcasting the sermon, with the remaining portion usually soliciting financial support in the way of donations or selling products. What products? You guessed it, the sermon. Thus, it is no surprise that the sermon has become the focal point of the worship experience for most believers.

The average time, according to the pastors interviewed and surveyed, spent on sermon preparation was 6-8 hours.[81] Interestingly enough, this is incongruent with our time management, when we consider the people's expectations. If preaching and teaching is the primary task, reason suggests, that this should be allotted the largest percentage of our time during the week. Of course, this is easier said than done. Point being, it is important that you are very intentional in setting aside time for sermon preparation, especially considering the already busy schedule most pastors carry. As I mentioned before, if you can get this time in place as your enter your first year, it is much easier than trying to carve it out later.

Two Lessons from the Greats

I would like to recommend two great books written by

---

[79] Corinthians 1:21

[80] Television Ministry Observation. by author. March 8-15, 2011.

[81] Virgil Woods. "Pastor Survey" via www.surveymonkey.com. Jan-Feb 2011.

Cleophus LaRue, Ph.D., Professor of Homiletics at Princeton Theological Seminary: *Power In The Pulpit*[82] and *More Power In the Pulpit*.[83] Dr. LaRue has gathered writings from a number of America's greatest preachers where they explain, in their own words, their sermon preparation process. As a bonus, each preacher also shares manuscript from one of his sermons. Allow me to share two of the many lessons offered in these reads. First, everyone's process was different. There is no cookie cutter approach that every pastor can apply and guarantee a great sermon. Some approaches were very systematic—choose text on Monday, study language on Tuesday, social history on Wednesday, rough draft on Thursday, illustrations on Friday, and finally prayer on Saturday. Others maintained a more open-ended process by which they wrote as so moved by the unction of the Holy Spirit. Both extremes have their advantages and disadvantages. What is more germane is that every great preacher had a process that worked for them and it is imperative that you develop a process that works for you. When time constraints abound, it is helpful if you are confident that your process will yield great results so that you don't feel pressured during preparation.

Secondly, a healthy devotional life is invaluable to the sermon preparation process. Those that maintained a healthy daily devotional life found that finding text, themes, topics and inspiration came without effort. A steady devotional life allows God to feed and guide your inner preacher as opposed to randomly choosing texts.

Listen to the words of Melvin V. Wade Sr., as quoted in More Power In The Pulpit:

> —There was one last piece in my evolving preaching regimen. Even though I was doing expositional preaching,

[82] Cleophus J. LaRue. *Power In The Pulpit*. (Louisville, Westminster John Knox Press, 2002).
[83] Cleophus J. LaRue. *More Power In the Pulpit*. (Louisville, Westminster John Knox Press, 2009).

I found that I was still reading my Bible only for sermon preparation. However, in 1999 I was diagnosed with leukemia, and with death staring me in the face—having been informed that bone marrow transplants for African American males were not that successful—I began for the first time reading the Bible devotionally.

I've since come to this start realization: that as witnessing follows worship, so biblical preaching follows biblical devotion…I would like to suggest that daily, private devotion is not some mere ineffective, optional extra. In fact, daily, private devotion should really be classified as an irrefragable, axiomatic sine qua non…private devotion is thus an irrefutable, obvious essential for any preacher.‖[84]

What form works best?

There is a lot to be said about preaching form, so much that there a number of good books that address this topic, take Thomas G. Long's book, *The Witness of Preaching*, for example. He states, and I wholeheartedly agree, that —A good sermon form, then, grows out of the particularities of preaching this truthful word on this day to these people.‖[85] Ultimately, *you* will have to decide what form is best suited for what occasion. When I speak at dinner banquets, I tend to be shorter and more direct. Why? Because, I know they tend to be long events and the speech is usually after the dinner, thus people are full and often lethargic, i.e. short attention span. When I preach funerals, I only quote one or two scriptures. Why? Because many people attending will not be regular church goers and quoting a thousand scriptures can be hard to follow, the jargon can make them feel out of place, and at the end of the day, they are

---

[84] Cleophus J. LaRue. *More Power In the Pulpit*. (Louisville, Westminster John Knox Press, 2009) Location 2618, Kindle e-book.
[85] Thomas G. Long. *The Witness of Preaching*. (Louisville, Westminster John Knox Press, 1989), 105.

not here for a scripture lesson in the same way Sunday worshippers are. When I preach an outside event, I always use their theme—no matter how crazy it may be. I have found this stretches my creative thinking and is always appreciated by those who invited me. When I preach one of the seven last words, it's always a one point sermon because there are usually time constraints. When I preach to youth, I tend to use more illustrations and humor as their attention span is usually more difficult to capture. When I preach outside of my normative cultural context, I talk slower. Why? Because I want to make myself more easily understood and I recognize that my —native‖ tongue may seem fast and confusing to those who are not accustomed to it. Where I preach and who I am preaching to always affects the form, content and presentation of my sermon.

Food For Thought

My goal here is not to provide an entire course on homiletics, rather to emphasize the importance of putting thought into your preaching and teaching as part of your ministry. I am confident, based on comments and suggestions of my congregants, that preaching is clearly my greatest strength. I have spent countless hours reading, studying and listening to great preachers. I want to close by offering eleven funny but very serious sayings I have learned along the way, we'll just call them *food for thought*.

1. —It aint got to be long to be strong!‖

I was once told that a good sermon is like a good skirt. It should be long enough to cover the topic and short enough to keep you interested. Some texts are very rich and there is always a temptation to preach everything you see. It is much better to end short and leave people desiring more than it is to over extend yourself and leave people wishing they could have gone home earlier.

2. —Good meat makes its own gravy!‖

Some preachers look so dynamic and entertaining it is awe-strikingly amazing. In an attempt to engage the crowd, it can be very tempting to lean on jokes and illustrations in your presentation. Though they do have their place in sermons and are often very effective in conveying a thought or idea, at the end of the day they are still ―gravy.‖ The real meat is God‛s word and this should be the substantive part of the sermon. The Bible is far from short of exciting stories. Don‛t get overwhelmed trying to make your sermon exciting. Trust me; the bible is intriguing enough by itself.

3. ―Borrow eggs, but make your own omelet.‖

I won‛t go as far as to say that it is impossible to preach someone else‛s sermon. I will say that it is never a good idea. Sermons are not just birthed out of study; they are complemented with our own personal convictions and experiences. From Paul to Peter, their greatest expositions were the ones they lived. I can flat footedly say that the most convincing sermons were not the ones I preached to the people, they were the ones I preached to myself. They were deeply rooted in my own history, experience and circumstance. It‛s ok to tell other people‛s story, but nothing is as convincing as your own.

4. ―Stick to the Point.‖

There is nothing worse than listening to a five minute illustration and asking yourself, what does this have to do with the text? I believe that you should be able to sum up your entire sermon in one or two sentences. Everything that is said should lend itself to this summation. If it does not, you risk losing the attention span of the people as they lose sight of your overall point or purpose.

5. ―K.I.S.S. – Keep it Simple Stupid‖

I am very familiar with the schematic of an opening, three points and a conclusion. Yes, this is very effective. Oftentimes, however, some of the most memorable sermons only have one point, that‛s why they are the most memorable sermons. They are easy to recall and remember. If you can't find three points to expound, instead try taking the time to thoroughly elaborate on the one point you do have.

6. —Open and Close

The introduction, in this author's opinion, and the close are the most important parts of the sermon. A good introduction will be intriguing and interesting enough that people will beg to hear more. Many good preachers start with modern day events or experiences, as opposed to the text, as a way to draw on people curiosity. The close is just as important as this is the last thing people hear and usually what they are most likely going to remember. Reiterating the major points of your sermon during the close is always a good idea.

7. —Do You

I know there are a lot of great preachers on television and in our communities, but God did not make you them, God made you as you are. I am a comedic person by nature, almost to a fault, so my sermons tend to be thoughtful, informative, yet very light hearted. Yes, there is a time and place for everything, including jokes, and some people frown upon the notion of being humorous during the preaching moment. However, I have found greater success in allowing my natural personality to flow through the presentation, than trying to be something that I know I am not. Remember, God knew who God called, when God called you.

8. —Be A Student of the Game

Think for a moment how many fights Muhammad Ali watched in preparation for his bouts. Think about how many football films NFL Championship teams study before they take the field. For a preacher, it is no different. Though conventional wisdom says study other preachers, I would like to go a step further. Anyone, who has mission of holding a crowd's attention for a period of time with nothing more than a microphone, is someone I can study. This means I am watching, politicians, comedians, talk show hosts, entertainers, lecturers, etc. I always ask myself, what is it that makes this person so captivating? Understanding that some things are not appropriate for the pulpit, I also seek what is to be gleaned from their presentation.

9. —Preach A Series, Not A Sermon‖

There is something special about preaching a multi-part series. Oftentimes, you will find one week less busy than another. This may be a good opportunity to write more than one sermon. A series also alleviates the temptation to preach every last single point you find in the sermon, as you know you can continue next week. Lastly, series can often draw congregants back another Sunday as they seek to hear more or the conclusion of the story.

10. —Know Your Audience‖

When I was asked to preach our Annual Conference sermon, I knew it would be a crowd of other preachers. I preached a sermon called —Bishop, I quit!‖ I used Elijah's desire to die as my text and talked about the frustrations of being a prophet. This sermon clearly would not have been appropriate for my congregation on a Sunday morning. We've said it once before, but I will say it again…It is important that you know who you are speaking to and tailor your message for such an audience. When accepting an outside speaking engagement, try as best as able to ascertain the audience you will speak to and write with them in mind.

11. —Where does the rubber meet the road?‖

So, what do people want in a good sermon? Here are some survey comments:[86]

---

[86] Virgil Woods. "Church Member Survey" via www.surveymonkey.com. Jan-Feb 2011.

—preaching and teaching the word in a way that is relatable to everyday life‖

—it helps me to examine myself and motivates me to be better‖

—relates biblical information and situations to present day terms‖

—how God's word is relevant to our current day life‖

I list this as the last and most important point, based on the survey and my own experience as a congregant and as a preaching pastor. The question looming in everyone's mind as they listen to a sermon is —What does this have to do with me?‖ In other words, how is this Sunday sermon going to help me Monday thru Saturday? Just as people are real, so are the issues and crisis they face every day. If a sermon does not speak to these issues, it is no more useful than a Band-Aid on your foot for a cut on your hand. Don't just preach the Good News, tell them why it's good for them today and how the lessons of antiquity articulate truths that are timeless.

Conclusion

Our survey showed that people come to hear an inspiring and informative sermon and it is your job to give it to them. Every sermon does not have to be —entertaining.‖ Some sermons ought to challenge, some sermons ought to intrigue, other sermons ought to make listeners feel good about being a Christian and still some ought to question the sincerity of the congregation's Christian walk. All in all, the most important thing is knowing that you have been faithful to preaching what God has placed on your heart.

Final Conclusion

My research clearly showed people's desire for a warm, welcoming church and pastor and their clear expectation of the church being a place to love and to learn. As you come into your first year, take advantage of the countdown period, use the resources as your disposal to begin learning the culture of your church. Establish a balanced diet of spiritual disciplines, positive self-expectations and sermon preparation time and show them the love you expect them to show others. And through it all, take your time. The areas identified in this research will be important for the duration of your ministry, not just the first year, so seek to strengthen and develop your understanding of each as you grow in your calling. You will make mistakes along the way, but learn from them, laugh at yourself every once and while and keep pressing for the Kingdom of God.

Bibliography

Alexander, Neil M. *CircuitRider*. V.33 No.1. Nashville: Cokesbury, 2008.

Ammerman, Nancy T. and Jackson W. Carroll, Carl S. Dudley, William McKinney. *Studying Congregations: A New Handbook*. Nashville, Abingdon Press, 1998.

Bass, Diana Butler. Christianity for the Rest of Us. SanFrancisco, Harper, 2006.

Bradt, George B., Jayme A. Check and Jorge E. Pedraza. *The New Leader's 100 Day Action Plan*. New Jersey, Wiley & Sons, 2009.

Crowley, Eileen. *Liturgical Art for a Media Culture*. Collegeville, MN: Liturgical Press, 2007.

Dickler, Jessica. "Stressful Jobs that Pay Badly." *CNNMoney.com*. http://money.cnn.com/galleries/2009/pf/0910/gallery.stressful_jobs/10.html.

Foster, Richard J. *Streams of Living Water*. New York: Harper Collins, 1998.

Hawn, C. Michael. *One Bread, One Body: Exploring Cultural Diversity in Worship*. Bethesda, MD: Alban Institute, 2003.

Judy, Dwight H. *Christian Meditation and Inner Healing*. Akron: OSL Publications, 2000.

Kim, Don. *World Evangelism*. Lecture from course taught at Garrett Evangelical Theological Seminary, Evanston, IL. January 2009.

LaRue, Cleophus J. *More Power In the Pulpit*. Louisville, Westminster John Knox Press, 2009.

LaRue, Cleophus J. *Power In The Pulpit*. Louisville, Westminster John Knox Press, 2002.

Law, Eric. H. F. *Sacred Acts, Holy Change.* Danvers, Chalice Press, 2002.

Lewis, Robert and Wayne Cordeiro. *Culture Shift: Transforming Your Church From The Inside Out.* SanFrancisco, Jossey-Bass Publishing, 2005.

Long, Thomas G. *The Witness of Preaching.* Louisville, Westminster John Knox Press, 1989.

Mancini, Will. *Church Unique.* San Francisco, Jossey-Bass, 2008.

Miller, James F. *Go Build A Church!* Enumclaw: WinePress Publishing, 2007.

Neff, Thomas J., and James M. Citrin. *You're In Charge, Now What?* New York: Three Rivers Press, 2005.

Nouwen, Henri. *Reaching Out.* New York, DoubleDay Press, 1975.

Palmer, Parker J. *Leading From Within: Let Your Life Speak, Listening for the Voice of Vocation.* Wiley & Sons, 2000.

Reiland, Dan. *Shoulder to Shoulder: Strengthening Your Church by Supporting Your Pastor.* Nashville, Injoy, 1997.

Scazzero, Peter. *The Emotionally Healthy Church.* Grand Rapids: Zondervan, 2003.

Schnase, Robert. *Five Practices of Fruitful Congregations.* Abingdon Press, 2007.

Stewart, Carlyle III. *Quarterly Review: A Journal of Theological Resources for Ministry,* Spring 2003, Article Titled: "Why Do Clergy Experience Burnout?"

Thompson, Marjorie J. *Soul Feast.* Louisville: Westminster John Knox Press, 1995.

Thurman, Howard. *Disciplines of the Spirit.* Richmond, Indiana: Friends United Press, 1963.

Waltz, Mark. *CircuitRider.* V.33 No.1. Nashville: Cokesbury, 2008.

Warner Brothers Entertainment. The Matrix Reloaded. DVD. Copyright 2003.

Warren, Rick. *The Purpose Driven Church.* Grand Rapids, Zondervan, 1995.

Watkins, Michael. *The First 90 Days.* Boston, Harvard Business School Publishing, 2003.

Made in the USA
Monee, IL
29 August 2023

41760128R00056